"Knowing the signals of love gives you an edge. The more you know about the rules and non-verbal idiom of attraction, the stronger your court-ship image will be."

—*Dr. David B. Givens*

Millions of men and women are searching for love, and simply don't know where—or more importantly, how—to look. But every time you walk into a restaurant, a supermarket, or a crowded bus, you're communicating unconsciously in a powerful, non-verbal language.

Now, renowned anthropologist David Givens explores the complex, intriguing world of courtship, seduction, and intimacy in a fascinating, sympathetic guide to the hidden meanings and messages we project in our search for love.

"Love Signals tells you exactly how to convey to the opposite sex, even someone you have never met, that you are available and interested. On every page you will learn something new and . . . compellingly practical."

Michael Morganstern, author of
How to Make Love to a Woman

LOVE SIGNALS
HOW TO ATTRACT A MATE

DR. DAVID B GIVENS

PINNACLE BOOKS NEW YORK

Excerpt from "On Your Own" by F. Scott Fitzgerald, in *The Price Was High: The Last Uncollected Stories of F. Scott Fitzgerald,* reprinted by permission of Harcourt Brace Jovanovich, Inc. Copyright © 1978 by Frances Scott Fitzgerald Smith. First appeared in *Esquire.*

Excerpt from "A Rotten Success Story: John Lydon of Public Image Ltd" by Frank Rose, reprinted by permission of the Virginia Barber Literary Agency, Inc. First appeared in *Esquire.*

LOVE SIGNALS

A Pinnacle Books edition, published by special arrangement with Crown Publishers, Inc.

Crown edition published in 1983
Pinnacle edition/February 1985

ISBN: 0-523-42431-0

Can. ISBN: 0-523-43343-3

Printed in the United States of America

PINNACLE BOOKS, INC.
1430 Broadway
New York, New York 10018

9 8 7 6 5 4 3 2

For Doreen

Acknowledgments

Barbara Grossman, Senior Editor at Crown Publishers, was indispensable to this project, as were my agents, Arthur and Richard Pine. I am deeply grateful.

I want to thank Foster Martin of Nevis Island, West Indies, for his editorial help and for the IBM Selectric II, a magnificent machine. Thanks are also due hundreds of unnamed men and women across the nation who let me watch and take notes on their wooing habits. (I was attacked only once.) I am indebted to certain people in San Antonio, Texas, the brewers of Lone Star beer, for helping me stave off writer's stroke, and to Sue Squire, whose expressive shoulders deserve special mention.

This book would have been impossible without help from a talented editor-turned-lawyer, Donna Holt. All beginning writers need someone special like Donna in their corner to help them do battle, *mano a mano*, with the belligerent written word. If she hadn't helped at every turn I'd never have made it through this cruel and unusual process.

Contents

Contents

Preface

I can never bring you to realize the importance of sleeves, the suggestiveness of thumbnails, or the great issues that may hang from a bootlace.

—SHERLOCK HOLMES TO WATSON

Attracting a mate can be harrowing at times, but it's not really hard. Men and women couple routinely, every day, and the human race keeps growing. Mother Nature went to a great deal of trouble to make our faces, bodies, and gestures appealing and revealing to the opposite sex. And we iced the cake with poetry, mascara, cologne, tube tops, love songs, and Mustang convertibles.

Sex appeal can be broken down, analyzed into nonverbal signals. Today, the most celebrated sexual signals are delivered by biceps, breasts, thin waists, eyes, and fannies. But there are hundreds more. To woo someone we might send and receive more than a thousand courtship signals. No one gets by on just muscles or an hourglass figure.

As far as I know, the biggest courting sign was erected in March, 1981 in Texas. It was larger than life; in fact, it was a billboard. In big letters a thirty-three-year-old man advertised, "Wife Wanted, New or Used, Kids OK." Thirty women answered the ad, but after a three-day courtship, one woman turned down the advertiser's marriage proposal because, she said, he was too pushy. The man had the right idea; we attract mates with *signs*, alright, but the best signals are considerably less blatant and more personal. Head-tilts, brow-raises, prominent cheekbones, soft voices, perfumes, scoop necks, soft sweaters, *en face* gazes, things like that. Not roadside signs.

All of us carry around enough gender signals on our bodies to attract a mate. Some people, like Farrah Fawcett or Burt Reynolds, have more than they absolutely need, but nobody is totally lacking in charm. Tom Thumb was only three feet, four inches tall when he married. Anna Swan was seven feet, five and one-half inches tall when she married Martin Van Buren Bates, who was shorter by three inches. Siamese twins Chang and Eng Bunker, joined at the chest, married sisters. Despite his disfigured face and frightfully deformed body, John Merrick, the famed Elephant Man, never failed for feminine companionship—including visits of royal ladies—in the last years of his life.

But, although anybody can attract a mate, it's important to attract the *right* mate. If the Sexual Revolution of the 1960s and '70s has taught us anything, it's that sex without feeling and involvement is a psychological dead end. Finding the right mate takes time and patience and discernment. Because it's no fun to wake up to find Mr. No Way or Ms. Definitely Wrong under the quilt, we go through a ritual period before commitment in which we test each other by exchanging signals of interest and affection. This in-between, getting-to-know-you span is *courtship*.

Now the word "courtship" may sound old-fashioned and summon up an image of grandparents spooning, sparking, and pitching woo on a porch swing. Even dictionary definitions sound quaintly out of date: "The act of wooin in love," or "Solicitation of a woman to marriage."

Nevertheless, courtship is flourishing in the 1980s. The time spent attracting a mate is as much a part of our lives now as it was at the turn of the century. No one taps on a stranger's shoulder and requests sexual favors, just like that. Only a rapist pursues sex without courtship. A decade after the much-exaggerated sexual revolution, people are courting as arduously and effectively as ever. Only the scenarios and the equipment have changed.

What Has Changed?

The most important change in contemporary courtship comes from the fact that there are more single people nowadays. Indeed, because more men and women between the ages of twenty-five and forty-four live alone than before, they have become known by the generic category "Singles." More people separate and divorce today than used to in Grandmother's time. The 1980 census shows that there are more than 21 million *nonfamily* households (mostly persons living alone)—72 percent more than there were in 1970.

The millions of singles searching for love have spawned some new institutions. There are health spas, or "total fitness centers" in the jargon, where singles can swim, play racquetball, and lift weights together and court in a frothing whirlpool tub. The singles' bar has come of age. Men and women have been meeting in taverns since the end of World War I, but today's singles-oriented lounges are . . . there's no other way to put it . . . *mind-altering*. Sophisticated, Disney-inspired themes (1700s pirate, 1800s sea captain, 1850s cowboy, 1930s Bogart—always the safe past) and sensory manipulating devices (Dolby sound; red-hued lighting; laser techology; narrow, "knee-brushing" passageways, masculine "club" atmospheres) calm, arouse, and synchronize guests as soon as they come through the doors. To enter a modern bar is to abandon all rationality and woo in an altered state.

For people who find random meetings with strangers

distressing there are a host of electronic courtship services: photo, video, and computer dating and radio call-in shows, as well as newspaper and magazine personal ads—all of which allow mate-seekers to court from a distance, spatially disconnected—safe, in a word. Sooner or later, even with these insulated techniques, men and women must face up to one another and exchange the tried-and-true wooing signals in person.

Winning the Right Mate

The whole idea of courtship is to win a mate who is right for you. But if "winning" also brings to mind the words "duel," "rivalry," "also-ran," and "runner-up" it's because courtship is fiercely *competitive*. Winning a mate may be the most competitive thing you ever do. Not only must you do battle man to man, or woman to woman, but you must also fight the opposite sex. In courtship it's man vs. woman in five savage rounds, or phases, each with its own rhythm, logos, and nonverbal language.

Knowing the signals of love gives you an edge. The more you know about the rules and nonverbal idiom of attraction, the stronger your courting image will be. And by understanding which signals tell when people are interested, you'll have more choice in the matter of whom to woo.

Flying Fists and Psychic Damage

I wrote this book five years after publishing an article in *Psychiatry* on "The Nonverbal Basis of Attraction: Flirtation, Courtship, and Seduction." The academic reaction surprised me. I got letters from around the world: from Japan and Australia, from every country in Western Europe, even from Eastern-Bloc countries and the USSR. Scholars from universities, psychiatric clinics, and medical centers everywhere seemed to be interested in courting and its nonverbal signs.

But my seduction study drew even more notice here in the United States. I was unprepared for the media attention the little article pulled. Most "scholarly" essays collect like newspapers in a pile and collapse under their own dry weight. But parts of this article went out on the AP and UPI wires, and calls came in regularly asking for telephone, radio, and TV interviews. For three years I was able to talk to people all over America, and courtship no longer seemed so academic.

Studying the signals of attraction takes you swiftly to the thin-skinned heart of self-esteem. There's nothing more personal than telling a woman why the shape of her cheek-bones or the pouty flair of her lower lip makes her attractive. And when you tell a man who carries his entire courting image in his pectorals that women's eyes don't automatically bounce like marbles when he takes his shirt off, you risk witnessing a demonstration of just how effective those pecs can be.

Once on "Donahue" I made a tactical error and commented on a woman's puffy sleeves. She and half the audience that summer morning had on dresses with puffed sleeves, and as I went on about how the roundness of the sleeve worked as a "frozen" submissive gesture, I noticed an ominous squirming in the studio crowd.

"How can you *say* that?!" the shocked young woman blurted into the microphone. Defensive antennae sprouted from a hundred coiffed heads, and a clear plastic screen seemed to drop in front of the stage. I'd inadvertently touched a collective nerve.

Most of what this book reports comes from direct field observations. To gather material I immersed myself in the singles' culture (which includes more than a few married people with liberal world views). I went where single men and women congregate and participated. With an Irish coffee in one hand and a spiral notebook in the other, I watched, and became what French anthropologist Claude Lévi-Strauss has called the alienated eye-witness.

Love Signals is part ethnography and part ''how-to.'' It documents the little courting rituals you see in elevators, in supermarkets, and on buses. And it suggests ways to gaze, ways to read eyes across a room, ways to sit, stand, align, posture, gesture, say the right thing, lift a drink, and successfully participate in the fascinating ritual of boy-meets-girl.

Love Signals

Introduction

She half consents, who silently denies.
—OVID

Friday P.M., Oct. 8—On the University of Washington campus, cool, light rain," my field notes read. No one was sitting on the damp, spongy lawn outside, so it was time to move the observations indoors. The lunch crowd in the cafeteria had thinned to one or two persons per table throughout the huge hall. As a rule, college students disperse and fill a space like gas molecules.

I sat and kept my eye on a cluster of tables, each occupied by a lone man or woman. I read the school paper and nibbled on a hamburger to reassure those around me that I was "safe." During her studies, primatologist Diane Fossey chewed on tropical leaves and belched noisily to calm skittish mountain gorillas in Rwanda. Eating shows animals you mean no harm. If it worked with apes it would work with students. And, to keep from threatening her gorillas, Fossey gazed away whenever they looked at her face. I did the same. When a man or woman caught me looking, I was careful not to glance away suddenly, which would connote I had been caught in the act. So I kept still and moved my eyes upward in their sockets to suggest something akin to deep thought.

The strategy paid off. Halfway through my burger, I saw an older graduate student, a scholarly type (academic beard, khaki pants, tweed jacket), put his food tray on the far corner of a co-ed's table. The young woman had a scholarly look, too (black tights, no makeup, hair in a bun). I sensed attraction, a hormonal flicker. But the courtship began slowly, like a Russian novel. It was a pattern I'd seen before.

At first, "Bun" and her partner, "Tweed," studiously ignored each other. Bun's upper body was angled away from Tweed, who sat turned away from her. No eye contact, not even a glance: each behaved as if the other radiated a protective psychic force field. Anthropologists call this avoidance phenomenon "establishing personal space." Getting used to closeness takes time.

Two minutes into lunch, Bun tendered the first beckoning cue. She took an art history book from her bag and set it noisily in the middle of the table. Then she turned her body toward Tweed and aggressively thumbed the pages. An amusing ploy . . .

But it was effective. Tweed shifted his weight and brought his shoulders into alignment with hers. Then, in an act of will, he broke through her psychic wall and gazed down at the open book. Too close for comfort, though, because he quickly looked away. Seconds later, he stretched, raised fisted hands to shoulder level, spread his elbows widely, yawned, and thrust out his chest. So . . . he *did* like her.

Unconsciously, Bun returned the gesture. She echoed the arm-flexing movement, stretched, and then thrust out her own ample chest. As Tweed and Bun's upper bodies moved in synchrony, like bodybuilders posing, they locked eyes for the first time. Tandem chest-thrusting can be deadly.

I took notes, but I could predict the outcome. Just after throwing out his chest Tweed commented on the art book, said something about Cézanne. Or was it Miró? It doesn't matter—topics rarely do—the important thing was that he spoke.

A serious conversation began. Bun and Tweed exchanged a torrent of courting gestures with the words. He smiled, her head tilted, he gazed down, her shoulders caved in, he drawled, she laughed, he touched, she purred, they paired, and wound up leaning in toward each other, faces not eighteen inches away. When they traded phone numbers on pieces of scratch paper I knew I was onto the real thing: courtship, American style. It was a lock.

What Is Courtship?

Courtship is an unrelenting, nonstop activity. Not just here on campus, but everywhere men and women gather. You could say human beings are *doomed* to court. Sooner or later almost every twosome gets boxed into courtship's gummy routines. We can't escape the sexual angle. It's always there, even though it's impossible to go the distance with everyone we court.

In *The Naked Ape* Desmond Morris calls man the "sexiest" primate. Unlike monkeys and apes, which breed seasonally, and sometimes just for a few weeks each year, human beings can make love in any season, at any stage of the menstrual cycle, even in late pregnancy. Men and women can make love in a tree, on a kitchen table, aboard a DC-10, on the steps of the Capitol—anyplace. In a recent *Ladies' Home Journal* survey, 18 percent of the religious, middle-income, college-educated readers confessed to making love in the family automobile!

Anytime, anyplace—but not with any*one*. People are more fastidious about partners than they are about time and place. They pick and they choose, and the selection process is *courtship*. Most of us identify courtship with attracting a mate, but it has an equally important flip side. Courtship attracts and repulses, says yes *and* no. It's a double-edge sword, a binary cutting device that rules in and rules out.

The most apt analogy is that of a screen. Courtship is like a semipermeable membrane, a sieve that separates coarse from fine. It chooses and refuses, but especially the latter—courtship keeps out more people than it lets in. Most courtships end in screen-out well before lovemaking has a chance to occur. A good thing, too; as Bertrand Russell once noted, without courtship we would soon face sexual exhaustion.

Signs, Signals and Displays

Courtship runs on *messages*—on physical signals and displays. Love may be intangible, but love communication is concrete, real. Before we make love we exchange come-hither cues that are mainly messages about proximity. Men and women swap wooing signs to close the distance separating them. Nearness, it goes without saying, is the key to copulation. Sexual intercourse makes physical closeness imperative.

The need for closeness necessitates courtship. Some animals, like the sardine-size fish called the California grunion, can mate without touching. The silver grunion female lays eggs, and the male fertilizes them after they're in the sand. As you would expect, grunion courtship is nothing to write home about. There's no need for wooing at all. But when animals must touch to mate, little dances and other rituals are necessary to bring them into range. Males and females do a slow schottische, signals go back and forth, distance closes—and mating becomes a short shot.

For many animals, success in wooing—sending just the right signs—is a matter of life and death. Consider the male wolf spider, who must get near enough to his short-fused mate to insert a sperm packet in her body. One too-eager footstep as he creeps down her earthen burrow and, imagining he is either predator or prey, she attacks him. Male wolf spiders must approach cautiously because the slowed motion itself is a courting signal. And when he meets her head-on in the dark he must reach out and stroke her just right or she kills him on the spot. This savageness is on a par with the atmosphere at some Manhattan singles' bars.

Wolf-spider courtship is grimmer than what you find in most species. But the cautiousness and slow motion, the gentle stroking—these qualities are found throughout the animal kingdom and in every human group. Caveman courtship, beating with clubs and dragging by the hair, never existed. Human courtship is cautious, gentle, and slow-paced in all known cultures.

Take the Cheyenne Indians of the Great Plains in the 1850s. A Cheyenne brave would stand silently with his head lowered alongside a maiden's usual footpath and wait timidly. As the maiden passed, the young man would freeze, statuelike, until she gave some faint signal recognizing his presence—a quick look from under her eyebrows, perhaps, or a brief smile. The brave's courage would build, and the next time she walked by he might gently tug on her skirt. Cheyenne courtship started just as human relationships begin almost everywhere—slowly, tentatively, and silently.

Nonverbal Cues

Worldwide, silence is the rule in the early stages of courtship. The first two steps—which we'll be calling

Phases One and Two—are in fact wholly preverbal. And even after speaking begins, the process relies on smell, touch, vision, and tone cues, all of which convey feelings more reliably than words do.

Courting signs are multisensory and nonverbal the world over. In Borneo, a Dusun woman gazes and angles her head to show her interest in a man. She won't reveal her feelings in so many words, but by touching the man's hands as she passes him a cup of rice wine at a party, a woman may silently invite sexual intimacy. It's like Mrs. Robinson's come-on to Benjamin in *The Graduate*.

Closer to home, at a fraternity-sorority keg party, men and women shell one another with a blitzkrieg of nonverbal cues. It's like parties everywhere. Each piece of clothing has a sexual significance, from the casual ankle-revealing "Tornado" sandals with braided straps to the soft (and touchable) lambswool sweater tied on over the shoulders. The students liberally adorn their bodies with visual and tactile gender signs. The sweet smell of Brut, the piercing, spicy aroma of English Leather, the floral fragrance of Ariane cologne—an olfactory collage greets your nose over the smell of spilled beer. Betty Boop-style stiletto heels tap out an ear-catching beat on the cedarwood deck. And that couple embracing behind the barbecue, the subtle swaying as they hold each other—that's a "vestibular" signal: the rocking motion pacifies and soothes, and helps make it easier for them to stay close.

We send and receive most love signals unconsciously. A woman might not understand why moving rhythmically side to side in a man's embrace is so relaxing, unless someone points out the calming "maternal" effect rocking has. A man might not realize that it's her repeated head-tossing, that upward jerk and shake of her head, that makes one particular woman seem more interested in him than in other men nearby.

Even though they are, for the most part, unconsciously

given and received, courting gestures work better than courting words. Nonverbal signals arouse the deeper parts of our brain where mating instincts lie. Facial expressions, body movements, and postures register in these primordial areas more directly and urgently than the sounds of speech. As sailors know, you need not speak the native tongue to flirt successfully. The language of love is universal.

A look at the brain's triune, or three-part, structure shows why men and women everywhere use the same courting signs. The outermost layer of our brain, known as the *neocortex,* is the rational, thinking part, the convoluted "gray matter" that enables us to add, subtract, speak, and ponder. Much of what goes on in the neocortex has to be learned—it's the part we educate in school—and much of what we are taught depends on the society we're born into. We learn English, and Athenians learn Greek, which can make talking about love awkward.

But our wooing cues come from two more-primitive areas in the brain, the mammalian *limbic system* and the archaic *reptilian core*. It's as if we had a live-in serpent and a resident furry mammal in our brain case making all the major courting decisions.

Most of our facial expressions, body movements, and postures come from these older reptilian and mammalian brains. This fact explains why our courtship resembles that of animals. It explains, too, why the mating game defies reason. Sex and thought are on separate levels, on different neurological floors. That's why we court impulsively and then spend months thinking about what happened.

The point is this. Wooing signals are "prewired" in our brain. No one needs to take a high school course in basic courtship to win a mate. We attract partners intuitively, instinctively, and unconsciously.

Few may realize, for instance, that around a handsome man women often unwittingly adopt what is known as the "coy look." Unthinkingly, even the most self-possessed

woman will bend her head down into a submissive posture
to make herself more appealing. First, she'll tilt her head
forward, as if she's looking down at her feet. Then, keeping her chin down she'll turn her head halfway to one side
so she can see her shoulder without straining her eyes.
Holding her head in this position she will at last look at the
man to whom she is attracted.

Coy looks combine *liking* (signaled by the direct eye
contact) with *submissiveness* (signaled by the angled, lowered head). A coy look says, in essence, "I like you and I
won't resist should you approach." And it says it effectively,
silently, and unconsciously.

Biologists have found the gesture even in lower branches
of the evolutionary tree, in the courtship of possums. The
possum is one of Earth's most primitive mammals, so
when you see possum cues you know you're dealing with
ancient roots. When a female possum isn't in the right
mood—when she doesn't feel like giving in to a male's
amorous nuzzlings or his repeated attempts to follow—she
turns on him and hisses, clicks her teeth, grabs him with
her hands, and if necessary bites him. But when she is
receptive she pitches her head down and turns her face
away at an angle to reduce the threat of her gaze. Her
glamorous coy look brings the male in like a magnet.

We'll find a host of submissive cues—like pigeontoeing,
shoulder-shrugging, palm-rotations, sideward head-tilts, self-
clasping, limb-flexing, and so on—ingrained in our mating
dances. Meekness is a theme in courtship because by
trading diffident signals, men and women give each other
permission to draw near.

Breaking the Stranger Barrier

But why does courtship need the indirectness of gestures,
postures, and coy looks? Why must our wooing be a

nonverbal cakewalk? What's wrong with saying something, coming right out with it in speech? Why can't a man just walk up to a woman, put himself forward and make an offer in *words?* Why can't a woman just sit down next to the man she's been eyeing and strike sparks directly?

Most bare-knuckle mating strategies don't work. Bald, head-on approaches generally scare people away, as the Texan's "Wife Wanted" billboard campaign did, a tactic that crossed a new frontier of bluntness in courtship. Straightforward approaches are counterproductive because they collide with a natural *stranger barrier,* an innate fear or wariness human beings have for one another. Any unfamiliar person—"the stranger in our midst"—is automatically feared, or at least mistrusted, until he proves himself safe.

It's as if we had a medium-size cyst of distrust lodged deep in our mammalian brain. Stranger anxiety is an indestructible part of human nature buried in the limbic system. Most of us experience measurable anxiety around an unfamiliar adult. Fearful reactions vary, but in most people the "fight-or-flight" symptoms are wet, cold palms, an increase in blood pressure, quickened breathing and heartbeat, and a churning stomach. A person automatically goes on guard around strangers; we have to give off a blizzard of friendly cues to court a wary man or woman.

Nature encoded the stranger-anxiety response in our genes. Three-month-old babies who have never had a bad experience with a stranger show fear when an unknown person approaches. A "threatening" man or woman—even the friendliest visiting aunt—can make an infant cry, face away, frown, pout, show his tongue, stare, grow suddenly serious, startle, gaze downward, tighten his lips, reach a hand behind the head, clasp his arms and legs, cling tightly to Mother, or pucker up his face like a squeezed sponge.

Neither the fear nor the body signals ever go wholly away. Stranger anxiety stays with us in varying degrees throughout life. The same pouts and tongue-shows leak negative feelings later in courtship. A person can mean no without saying it. The closer an unfamiliar person gets, the louder the neural alarms. When a stranger at a party leans over and touches your knee a Klaxon sounds. And at superclose range, within the tolerance of sexual intimacy, even your best friend can feel like a stranger.

All of which is why we need courtship. Courtship, the special ''getting-acquainted'' period, helps break down our body's natural barriers to physical intimacy. Every shy glance, honeyed voice, and warm, winning smile helps reduce the body space separating mates-to-be. Couples exchange nonverbal signs, nearness grows, and at a given stage in the courting progression lovemaking is unavoidable. After courtship, what started out as a 400-yard, par-5 hole becomes a 2-inch putt.

Phasing into Intimacy

No golfer expects a hole in one. In golf a player approaches the green gradually in a sequence of shots. And it's the same in courtship. The transition from stranger to lover moves through five distinct phases: Attention, Recognition, Speech, Touch, and Lovemaking. But at this point the golf analogy collapses, because few would-be lovers ever make it all the way to the hide-a-bed. Unlike the game of golf, where everyone makes it to the cup eventually, in courtship most people get screened out before the Touch Phase.

Phase One—*Attention*

All the smiling, firm handshakes, excited greetings, nervous laughter, clown-colorful costumes, and scurrying about you see at parties can be viewed in a detached way as *attention* signals. Phase One, the Attention Phase, is reduced to three messages: (1) presence ("I am here"), (2) gender ("I am man/woman"), and (3) harmlessness ("I won't hurt you").

Men cough, swagger, tell jokes, and stand tall. Women wear hard heels that clomp, pleated dresses that sway, and perfumes that fill and define their space. Men swell up and occupy fixed personal territories. Women move restlessly back and forth. Presence is announced. Women wear frilly tops, lace-trimmed dresses, and pearls; men wear shoulder-enhancing sportcoats and sportshirts with wide-open collars to display the masculine neck. Both sexes play up the body's natural gender signs, and the contrasts between male and female are communicated. But no one is touching, and few get close enough to even smell each other's carefully chosen cologne—harmlessness is established.

Phase Two—*Recognition*

As she broadcasts her attention cues, a woman reads men's reactions at the same time. Communication in the Recognition Phase has an essential radarlike quality. It's a little like a bat's sonar—as a woman moves through a courting space, at a singles' bar, say, she bounces her attention-getting signals off the assembled men and reads what they give back. She'll swoop in close to men who emit "soft," positive echoes and give those with "hard," negative vibrations a wide berth.

Men do the same. A man sitting across from a woman in an office-building cafeteria, for example, simultaneously gives and reads cues. The woman won't tell him how she feels in words so he takes a nonverbal reading: Does she glance at him or turn away? Does she coyly tip her head forward or throw it disdainfully back? And so on. Of course, he won't consciously tally up the cues (like the low-profile anthropologist is doing there behind the potted palm), but all her gestures and movements, or even the lack of these, will automatically register on the toteboard in his unconscious brain.

In Phase Two a subtle, "Clever Hans" psychology is at work. Clever Hans, a horse, astounded scientists of his day by tapping out answers to math problems with his hoof. Asked how much is four and four, Hans would tap eight times. Crowds were amazed by the horse's seeming brilliance.

What really happened was this: Hans "read" audiences so astutely he picked up subtle body cues telling when he should *stop* his tapping. A questioner would unthinkingly raise his brows, lift his chin, or go up on his toes on Hans's next-to-last stomp, and Hans would respond by stopping.

Recognition Phase cues come from the lower mammalian and reptilian parts of our brains rather than from the neocortex. For all its worth in courtship, you might as well check your reason at the door. When scientists removed the neocortex of a female hamster, for example, it left her without the intelligence to find her way out of a maze. But she still sent all the right wooing signs, was receptive to a male, gave birth to eight pups, and was a good mother.

Phase Three—*Speech*

Speaking is the most difficult test. Most people are screened out as soon as they open their mouth. Not only does a person lose the natural poise that silence itself carries but conversation gives clear information about education, social standing, and heretofore concealed mental quirks. But as important as words are, facial expressions, gestures, and postures in this stage are perhaps even more crucial.

Because of the close quarters and intimate eye contact of face-to-face conversations, you quickly feel one way or the other—warm or cool, rarely just neutral—about a partner. The strain of speaking puts physical closeness to its first big test.

With practice you can determine which conversations in a room will move ahead to Phase Four. For example, a conversation may seem friendly and flirtatious on the surface, but close analysis can reveal a fatal flaw. I remember a chat between a young blond woman and an equally young, bland-but-eager military type. It looked like courtship at first, because they were smiling and laughing and really seemed to delight in each other's company.

But something was wrong. Although they had aimed their faces at each other—gaze was direct and eye-to-eye, and the planes of their faces were held in parallel—their torsos never fully squared up, not once in twenty minutes. She did not turn her shoulders toward him, just her face. The young woman's body was saying: keep your distance. She covered her mouth with her hand, an unfriendly cue in this setting, and a tenseness showed around her lips. Whenever he leaned in too close, she reacted with telling lip-compressions and tongue-shows, both negative stranger-anxiety signals, as if she felt him pressing in on her. She never gave him any chest-protrusions, head-tosses, hair-preens, or other flirtatious gestures.

Despite her apparent friendliness he ended up spending a lot of time and talk for naught; for eventually she stood and left without him. Had he known the meaning of the signals she was giving he might have turned his attention more successfully to another woman.

Phase Four—*Touching*

Couples who make it through the Conversation Phase shift into a tactile mode of communication. At this time courtship takes a quantum leap toward intimacy. Touching, our most ancient sense, predates hearing, sight, and smell by millions of years. Hugging is more than pleasant, therefore—it's primordial.

Before lovemaking, a couple needs tactile reassurance. At lovemaking proximity our bodies need more than words to be convinced everything will be OK. So before getting under the quilt couples get physical and lay on hands. They stroke, pat, hold, rub, embrace, pinch, tickle, wrestle, wash, carry, nuzzle, mouth, lick, bite, and kiss each other before folding down the sheets and fluffing up the pillows.

Analyze touch cues and you find an unmistakable parent-child flavor. Lovers on a park bench will use every tactile gesture found in the maternal-child bond. They mother each other, as it were. The same facial snuggles and rhythmic rocking movements, the same *en face* gazes, pet names, and baby-talk tones mothers use emerge, unmodified, in courtship.

Why the mother-child metaphor? That intimate, familial style starts an arousing feedback cycle that can bring a couple so physically together that sexual intercourse will seem like the world's most natural and unavoidable next step. Infantile cues stimulate parental cues, and the mothering treatment brings out infantile signals. It's the body's own circular reasoning, courtship's primal loop. Because of this, and the fact that with all the hands-on activity the erogenous zones jump for joy, Phase Five can sneak up on a couple before the pair knows what hit them. At this stage nature will permit no reasoned cry to interfere.

Phase Five—*Making Love*

Courtship leads to mating, coitus, copulation, sexual intercourse—call it what you will—and wooing ends when people make love. Few courtships, however, get this far.

Most relationships get screened out earlier in the progression.

After making love, a pair "spaces out," not in a drugged but in a spatial sense. After loving, a man and woman will put distance between themselves. They will sleep, leave, shower, smoke cigarettes, or go about their separate tasks. You will notice, too, that from the lovemaking stage on, couples will trade ever fewer courting signals. Some people say it's because the "magic" goes out of the relationship. Maybe so, but I doubt it. A better reason is that they have less need after Phase Five to negotiate closeness. The circuit has closed, and nearness is not the problem it was before. You can pick out mated pairs because in their ease with each other they take the distance for granted.

Men and women sometimes say, "We can keep it casual." But they don't understand courtship. Just as free lunches are hard to come by, free love—sex without dues—hardly exists. The special communication of lovemaking itself, the intimacy, the honey-coated caresses, the face-to-face, pelvis-to-pelvis, whole-body contact, can have certain unanticipated effects. Sex can obligate; the exchanged courting signals can forge a love bond that is not easily broken.

Quiz

- At a garden party you notice that men seem to walk stiffly and swagger when they arrive. The swagger means:
    a. "I am here."   b. "I am male."   c. "I am macho."
- When you find yourself gazing downward while talking with a handsome man or a beautiful woman, you're saying, in effect:
    a. "I am harmless: you may approach."
    b. "I'd rather not speak to you."
    c. "I've got something to hide."
- Which of these postures means someone is interested in you?
    a. "Pigeon toes."
    b. A sideward head-tilt.
    c. Self-clasping.
- To show availability and attract attention at a singles' bar, a woman should:
    a. Flex, pitch, and roll her shoulders.
    b. Keep her upper body motionless.
    c. Present her best profile and toss her head.
- To present the right masculine image, a man should lift his chin, square his shoulders, and puff out his chest. True or false?
- The best place to set up your "zone of radiance" at a party is:
    a. In the most congested area.
    b. Away from the crowd.
    c. Outside on the porch.

16

1

Phase One—Attracting Attention

It's better to be looked over than overlooked.
—MAE WEST

The attention phase is a restless and sometimes rowdy period. Men show off for women, and women display themselves for men. Gender advertisements range from bashful to rude, from reined-in to let-out, from Julie Andrews timid to Mae West rash, from Radar O'Reilly cautious to Burt Reynolds brash.

Attention Phase cues work to make a person's physical presence known. Before a man and a woman can get close enough to make love, they need to know that the other person exists. This may seem self-evident, too philosophically primitive even to bring up, until you grasp the just-as-basic fact that courtship is *competitive*. It is, in fact, one of life's nastier games. A person may have everything going his or her way—looks, intelligence, an American Express Gold Card—but until others *see* these appealing qualities, until their existence is known, they don't count. In courtship nothing works until it *shows*. And the showing must be *subtle* to work.

Lure, not Seize

Courtship operates on a principle of *luring*. Instead of chasing, cornering, and capturing a mate, instead of using force, we emit "come-hither" signals and sit back and play what amounts to a waiting game. Lure, not seize, is the rule. The idea is to draw partners in close with a lure first. Get them within eighteen to forty-eight inches and *then* go into the more intimate, face-to-face courting routines.

The most exotic luring technique of all is that of the satin bowerbird of Australia. The black, robin-size bowerbird male builds a ground nest out of thin sticks. About twelve inches high and open at both ends, the nest looks like a corridor or a stall. By itself, sitting on the sand, a nest is no more impressive than two clumps of bunch grass. But the bird adds on a little, flat twig porch, which he decorates to within an inch of its life with snail shells, pebbles, blossoms, and feathers, and if near a town, with cast-off plastic buttons, shards of crockery, empty shotgun shells, pieces of glass, ballpoint pens, marbles, and tin lids. With its gaudy front porch a bowerbird's nest is so attractive, so appealing, so sublimely seductive to the females that one will walk in on her own. She will stand in the corridor facing the display, the odd objects, and then courtship shifts into its face-to-face stage.

The idea in the Attention Phase is to beam out an irresistible message just like the bowerbird, and bring someone within your "zone of radiance"—the area that extends from eighteen to forty-eight inches in front of your body—where your face, eye, and body signals transmit most persuasively.

Human Bowerbirds

Long-distance luring accounts for much of what goes on in today's singles' bars. Take Monkeyshines, an Irish-theme restaurant and de facto singles' establishment in Seattle. On Friday nights the young professionals or "YPs," the twenty-five-to-forty-year-olds in three-piece suits and clingy dresses come to Monkeyshines to court and be courted. Voices boil up in the crowd as singles drink piña coladas under lazy wicker-and-walnut-bladed fans, tear-drop ceiling lights, and clubby prints of Englishmen in hunting pinks. Enthusiastic greetings, earnest small talk, and overzealous laughter—a constant, droning loudness—fills the room. At first the noise is upsetting. But after a glass of your favorite beverage you relax and begin to notice Attention-Phase cues ricocheting off the walls.

Over at the three marble-topped tables in the middle of the barroom you'll see several men standing and drinking at respectful distances from one another. They never say anything, just stand there silently, strangers, drinking and watching and . . . *posturing*.

These unpaired men, here week after week, are the girlwatchers of Monkeyshines, the bowerbirds. Fiercely costumed, they work the passive lure. Each man expects that on the strength of his appearance, his physical charm, such as it is, and on his clothing, his stance, the way he leans, the way he smokes, the cool way he looks around and sips beer, that he might attract an available single woman to come drink by his side. Not drink and talk, not yet, just drink and stand near at first so he might work in close to the horns, which is to say, send short-distance cues that could *lead* to talking.

Two of the loners take the lure a bit further. One man in a lime-green shirt has an eye-catching book, *Finding Money*, in front of him. The other man, wearing a faded denim jacket, a toothpick in his mouth, is reading the *Wall Street Journal*, also rich in money symbolism—and his reading is extremely intense. He holds the paper in both hands, six inches from his face, and his eyes move quickly back and forth over the page. The jean jacket and the *Journal*—an odd juxtaposition; and he's so absorbed a woman could slide in beside him without having to say anything. "Toothpick" is so wrapped up he's easier to approach than the more watchful men. Because of this he's the first to lure a woman into his territory, his "bower," and the first to engage in serious courting.

Luring is a bit like Zen—maddeningly indirect. The more energy a person puts into showing off, the harder it is to draw anyone near. Watch the Attention-Phase routine performed by "Leather Vest," who has put so much into his lure that he not only fails to attract women into his personal space, but in fact, sends them away.

Leather Vest swaggers into the bar and claims, with a flurry of quick gestures, a small round table near the window. He tosses his cigarette pack on the tabletop with a cool flick of the wrist and then picks the pack up again and takes out a Camel. Vest drums it on his thumb—involves his whole upper body in the movement—lights the cigarette and wags the match out with a flourish, as he exhales a little cannon burst of smoke. Without a word he has announced, "I am here."

Leather Vest has on a brown plaid shirt, open at the neck, and form-fitting Brittania jeans. A little Union Jack insignia situated high on his buttocks calls attention to his derriere. The criss-crossing lines of his shirt help catch the eye, as does the contrasty centerpiece of his costume, a shiny, chocolate-brown cowhide vest.

Constantly "dancing"—changing position, shifting weight, fidgeting with his hands—Vest restlessly works his lure. But women stay away. Impatient, he does an about face and leans back against the table and rests his elbows behind him on the marble. He gazes on the singles at the bar, almost challenging them to look back.

When his tequila sunset arrives, he keeps his wrist rigid and uses his whole arm to stir the drink. He lifts it to his mouth as if he's curling a small training weight. He tosses his head, conspicuously smokes another cigarette, sits down, stands up, twirls, flexes, glares . . . and so it goes for half an hour. Vest stands in his little strutting ground like a sage grouse, gesturing for all he's worth, drinking and watching and posturing. Every movement has some body English or curlicue added on. He lures, but no women approach.

On analysis, Leather Vest's Attention-Phase signaling was one-third off. He was OK on two points—he let people know that he was *present* and that he was *male*—his act missed completely on the third. Vest didn't let women know he was vulnerable; he gave off nothing to show *harmlessness*.

His manic, overdone movements were too obviously put on. The weightlifter's drinking technique—unnecessary in the first place—should have been counterbalanced with softening cues, with a downward gaze, a sideward head-tilt, a self-clasping movement (pinching the earlobe, for instance), or a clumsy mannerism—anything to show he was accessible and wouldn't bite. Even his courting territory was forbidding, much too exclusive for a woman to enter easily. To walk over to Leather Vest's secluded spot would be to admit sexual interest. He should have set up his zone of radiance at one of the longer, more sociable middle tables, where women could approach without giving themselves away.

Presence—"I Am Here"

Nowhere in America is the Phase One message, "I am here," announced more stridently than it is on Greek Row.

You couldn't ask for a better place to study the human mating dance. Each spring as the chestnut trees leaf out and the rhododendrons bloom in fraternity-house yards, rock music booms out of dormer windows and off roofs, extremely amplified, like a hail of stun grenades. Loud music extends the psychic frontier of a fraternity house, makes the courting territory seem larger, and attracts female ears. It's a male thing, like birdsong. The sororities play their own, softer music indoors.

On Greek Row in spring the parking strips, sidewalks, and lawns swarm with moving bodies. A person is more noticeable outside than inside, of course, and to embellish visibility the young men and women amble, walk, jog, come here, go there, *move*, in a word, to catch the eye. They spend a lot of time being outdoors and underway without really having a destination. The Greeks seem to understand at an intuitive level that the eye is hypersensitive to motion. Our eyes can pick up the slightest visual shift, see a fly thirty feet away on a window pane when it moves. The human eye was designed to pick up movement, and anything in a fixed position quickly becomes boring.

Courtship clothing, too, makes special appeal to the senses. On Greek Row men and women wear bright, high-contrast tops that are as perfectly adapted to grabbing attention as tiger stripes. Greek shirts, blouses, vests, and sweaters bear little resemblance to the drab "sackcloth" and monk-academic tops worn by graduate assistants and others who are less involved in boy-meets-girl.

The noise, motion, and costumes of Greek Row boil down to the collective announcement, "We are here." The next step is establishing just who "we" are. . . .

Gender Advertisements—"I Am Man/Woman"

It's nice to know that someone has arrived at the Phi Mu toga party, but we also need to know, before courting, to prevent embarrassment, whether the new arrival is a man or a woman. Luckily, nature provides us with such a bounty of gender signals that recognizing a person's sex is rarely a problem.

Our faces and bodies contain more built-in sexual contrasts than you might realize. Take eyebrows, for example. Bushiness is not the whole story. A woman's eyebrow rides higher over her eye than a man's does. Whereas the male eyebrow hugs the bony eye orbit (the ridge of bone around the eye socket) and closely follows its contour, the female eyebrow—you can run your fingertip over it and feel the difference—starts out on the same ridge close to the nose, but flares up and off the ridge as you move out toward the ear.

The difference is subtle, but it makes a man's eyes seem more deeply set. And this gives him a somewhat sterner, more serious look. Because her eyebrows frame a larger patch of skin, a woman's brow line makes her eyes seem bigger. The lifted appearance gives her face a perennial look of surprise and "innocence." So not only does the eyebrow contrast convey, "I am male" or "I am female" but the feminine brow, which is less "fierce" than the masculine version, makes it easier for a man to approach. Even at rest a woman's eyebrows say, "I am harmless."

Differences between males and females are known as "sexual dimorphism." Animals, too, need to know a partner's sex before mating. So nature made sure her males and females differed in size, smell, form, color, markings, and behavior. Her method is to start with a female prototype and add on as many manes, combs, spurs, horns, crests, tusks, wattles, dewlaps, whiskers, topknots, muscles, antlers, and gular pouches as necessary to make male-or-female perfectly clear.

Humans are less sexually contrastive than, say, gorillas. A 450-pound silverback male can weigh twice what a female gorilla weighs. But we are more sexually dimorphic than parakeets. You can turn that bird every which way in your hand and still not know if it's male or female. Men and women are moderately contrastive, it turns out: somewhere between the gorilla and the parakeet.

On Greek Row, with the long-awaited arrival of sun and warmth, sexual and gender signals are tauntingly exhibited in sunbathing rituals. Sorority women make an art form of lying on a towel. Choosing the most conspicuous spot on the front lawn, close to the street and as far away as possible from the front door (so she can make a show out of getting a soda), a sister will unfurl her flapping signal towel in the breeze and bend over to smooth it out, just so, on the grass. The adjustment can take a while, giving her traits time to show. The hot-pink bikini hides her breasts and bottom the way dayglow orange hides a traffic cone. Bikinis capture the essence of courtship because they call attention to what they hide.

Next comes the oiling. Sorority women spread cocoa butter on their thighs and shoulders, as tribal New Guinea girls do, and sit out front displaying their glistening bodies to passersby. What helps the gender display work its magic is this: a sorority girl won't keep still. She and all her sisters on the lawn stay in motion—adjust their straps and tie their ties, fetch ice, borrow mist bottles, pay visits, brush their hair, file their nails, and reposition their towels. They don't court lying down.

Meanwhile, fraternity boys take off their shirts, cinch up their gym shorts, and put on muscle displays. It's not good form to stand and pose like the Incredible Hulk in front of the sunbathing crowd. Strategically, flexing biceps, quadraceps, and abdominals is out. But the brothers don't pump iron all winter for nothing. A subtler approach is to engage in a game of Frisbee.

Courtship Frisbee hardly resembles the casual, relaxed game you associate with easy summer days in the park. Courtship Frisbee is not a friendly game but a martial art, a form of man-to-man combat. Brothers take crouched stances near the sunbathing lawns, or on them, and rifle the mean, spinning disks at one another in bullet-flat arcs. The courters gradually stand farther and farther apart and go for distance, often grazing the heads of sisters who pretend not to notice.

Power and accuracy are the main criteria, as you might expect. Demonstrations of strength and control in throwing—hurling boomerangs, shotputs, weighted sticks, hatchets, axes, javelins, and spears—has been a masculine courting technique for thousands of years all over the world.

Throwing has deep roots in ancient hunting customs. Thirty thousand years ago hunting was necessary for survival, and women admired an accurate throwing arm. Today, it's hard to imagine anything but a vague, metaphysical link between Frisbee-throwing and courtship, until you try to picture a group of Future Accountants of America on a lawn showing off their finger speed on calculators. Frisbee gives young men a way to display strength and physical prowess. Women still admire vigor. The desperate running leaps, the impossible catches behind the back on stiffened index fingers, the derring-do of playing in traffic—Frisbee has it all. Years from now Valentine cards might show Cupid with a quiver of disks instead of arrows.

"I Am Harmless"

Being present and obviously male or female, however, is not enough. Before approaching an unfamiliar man or woman, a person needs to know the anticipated partner will be hospitable. People need to be reassured that partners won't be surly or gruff. They need clear, readable signs of *harmlessness*. Anyone who seems even latently unfriendly, which is to say anyone who does not actively go out of the way to disclaim hostility, will keep people who want to come closer away.

It's the same in animal courtship. To come on too strongly, too directly, or too soon only scares partners away. So baboons "grin" before approaching to groom one another. Organ-grinder monkeys "pout" before making advances. Dogs wag their tails to court, or curl them under to be courted. Animals, like humans, broadcast "friendly," threat-disclaiming signs to be sociable. When a cat's tail springs straight up like a kitten's, you know the cat won't scratch the hand reaching out to pet it.

Signs of meekness and humility are essential in our courtship, too. The harmlessness-connoting signal itself though, strictly speaking, is not attractive—only gender cues draw—but the vulnerability cue gives recipients permission to come near. This is why women find it easier to approach, say, an imposing pro football player at the next table if he has a cast on his foot and a crutch under his chair. Even the naked toes curling out of the plaster make him seem vulnerable, harmless, and psychologically accessible. Canes, casts, slings, limps, compression bandages, and so on, all signs of weakness, make a person easier to approach because they give viewers an edge of superiority.

The Shrug. The best universal threat-disclaimer is the shoulder shrug. Raising the shoulders is a gesture of uncertainty, submission, and "safeness." You can say, "I give up," anywhere on Earth by lifting your shoulders, tilting your head sideward, and rolling up your palms.

Without thinking, men and women pitch and roll their shoulders with partners they're attracted to. It's a way of showing personal harmlessness. Children know the light-voiced, meek approach works better than straightforward demands. When they lift their shoulders, tilt their heads, gaze down, and pirouette to ask you for candy at the store, you have to give in. They're so cute. . . .

The same principle works in courtship. When you elevate your shoulders a little—women can raise theirs higher than men can—you automatically seem less dangerous. It's because the shrug is a remnant of the protective startle reflex. Make a loud noise near a baby and as part of the innate startle reflex he will lift the shoulders. In a root sense, the shrug posture tells the person near you that because you're mobilized to protect yourself you're not going to attack.

Of course it's all subliminal. But you've seen exaggerated, burlesque versions of shrugging put on by actresses like Marilyn Monroe, Mae West, and Jessica Lange. Most women use shrug gestures in courtship, and if you watch for them you'll be surprised you never saw them before. Men shrug, too, and if you've ever wondered what it is women like about Phil Donahue, well, it's partly that he carries a potent magnetism in his shoulders. Donahue *courts* his guests, in effect, as he comes at them with his microphone, blue eyes, and rolling shoulders, and they'll say things on his show they wouldn't tell their best friends.

If shrug gestures say "I'm harmless," squared, military-style shoulders can say "I'm threatening." A lineup of soldiers all raising their shoulders wouldn't look forceful on the parade ground. It would almost seem like a chorus line. What makes a squared, shoulders-back carriage seem fiercer than the shrug posture? The former harks back to an inborn bluffing pattern and carries an innate menace. Preschool boys, for example, raise up to their full height, puff out their little chests, jut their chins forward, and pull their shoulders back as a bluff signal to show toughness vis-à-vis other little boys. It's a panhuman threat stance.

In a singles' bar you'll always see a few men posturing with military shoulders. They're the ones who stay alone all evening. What they're doing is showing strength to the *men* in the bar. Unfortunately, the projected power doesn't attract women. All military shoulders show is latent hostility and stiffness.

Men should avoid "Napoleonic" postures. Napoleon posed with his shoulders squared and his arms held against his sides. The emperor's upper body had a rigid, restrained appearance, proud but a bit harsh for courtship. A better way to stand is with your hands on your hips, relaxed. This automatically brings your shoulders forward, makes them friendlier. And the angular akimbo position of the arms held out away from the body makes for higher visibility. On a barstool, a man should lean forward a little, rest his right hand on his right thigh, and put his left hand in his pocket. This will raise his left shoulder, flex the right one forward, and create a softer symmetry.

He should keep his shoulders relaxed and his eyes up. Responsive eyes attract instant attention because a brief glance shows a woman he's taking her personally. He should be bending slightly forward when he's sitting in a chair, loosening his shoulders, clasping his hands in his lap, and meeting faces with a head-on gaze—without staring. Women will notice the displayed hands, which have an appeal of their own, and his relaxed pitched-forward shoulders will give him a sensitive, "yielding" look. Broad shoulders are attractive, of course, but flexing and dipping them at close quarters make it easier for women to draw near.

Head-Tilting. Head-tilting is a part of the shrug display. Open any popular magazine, like *Cosmopolitan*, to the ads and you'll see women's heads tilting over left or right as they model, hold, demonstrate, lay upon, or sit in an advertised product. The theory is that whatever is advertised, from liquor to shoes, the head-tilt will make someone more "approachable." Or browse through *People* and note how many more women than men have their heads canted over. Like raised shoulders, the tilt communicates an attitude of coyness. Tilts are most obvious in greetings. Studies show women tilt significantly more than men when they say hello.

But in courtship meetings, both sexes tilt. When you make eye contact with an unfamiliar man or woman to whom you're attracted, add a head-tilt. That simple gesture, and a smile, will make you seem friendlier than you'd seem keeping your eyes on the horizontal. Not only does tilting reduce the ambient threat, it also shows you're interested. People automatically cant their heads over when they listen to someone they really enjoy talking to. The tilt shows they're truly absorbed.

Avoid backward head-tilts. Nothing will make you seem more aloof, haughty, or disdainful than looking down your nose. You can experience the effect of this gesture by consciously tipping your head back and carrying your face just a few degrees higher than normal. (It's the posture you sometimes see bifocal wearers use.) Next time you talk with a friend, give that person a slight backward tilt and see what happens. Note puzzled reaction and your own odd, supercilious feeling. Something will seem wrong, because just a tiny down-the-nose posture is enough to make you seem insufferably arrogant. "Over the nose" is a pancultural sign of superiority that's best used to turn *off* a partner's ardor.

Pigeon-Toeing. Few people realize that the position of their feet—toed-in or toed-out—changes with a partner's social status. Watch shoes at the next office party, and you'll quickly understand the body language of feet. When the boss pats Bob on the back, watch Bob's feet pigeon-toe inward. The boss's will toe out. Then watch Bob's feet when he talks to his subordinates in the corporate pyramid—his own shoes will now toe out.

Watching feet helps you know where a person stands in

the pecking order. The meek invariably take the toes-in posture, because pigeon-toeing is yet another component of the larger shrug display. It, too, is a fragment of the protective startle reflex.

In courtship, both men and women unwittingly pigeon-toe. Tandem pigeon-toeing is, in fact, one of the first signs you'll see in couples where both partners obviously like each other from the start. But solitary women can use the posture consciously to attract men. That is, a woman can toe in a bit on purpose to show a man she'll accept his advances. A man, however, does better standing in the military, oblique position (heels closer together than toes), a sign that he is not cowed by other men. Courtship is harder for men because they must show a proper blend of harmlessness and strength.

"Unfolding." As you become more observant, you'll note that our bodies transmit clear information about confidence and fear. Anxious people tend to fold up their arms and legs—bend their elbows, hold their arms closely into their bodies, sit with their legs tightly crossed, and so on. Folding up shows they're ill at ease, mildly scared.

Confident people carry their arms and legs in more relaxed positions. You'll see less bend in the elbows and less ankle-over-ankle intertwining. Basically, the socially fearful person is folded and the self-assured is unfolded.

The unfolded postures work best in the Attention Phase. Note how you stand and sit when you're relaxed, by yourself watching TV for example, and bring these "looser" postures with you to social events. Tightly folded, "held-in" positions of the arms and legs can make you seem unwilling to participate.

No one needs an ultraconfident, suave stance to attract a mate. Indeed, you don't want an overly selfcontained air, which will only make you look conceited. It's OK to scratch, tug at an earlobe, and pinch the loose skin at the front of your neck. Just don't collapse in on yourself and fold up.

Send Clear Cues

We have seen that the first stage of boy-meets-girl is a period for attracting attention. Phase One is a time to let people know that you're present, a man or a woman, and unthreatening. We go through the Attention Phase before touching or kissing or fondling because that's how Mother Nature patterned our courtship, as well as the courtship of animals. Take the mating dance of the mallard duck for example.

To court a hen, a drake must (1) attract her attention and let her know he's interested; (2) show he is truly a male; and (3) defuse her aggression so she won't bite him. The male duck must send all three messages simultaneously, whether his mate is flying, swimming, walking, or standing on the shore. In a pond crowded with rivals, he has to pepper her continually with quacks and energetic body movements. It can take as much out of a duck as it takes out of a man.

Anyone who has ever seen a duck pond in mating season may have wondered if somebody put something in the water to trigger the berserk chasing, flapping, odd, bobbing head movements, and curious neck-stretching. In spring the normally quiet pond becomes a frothing tangle of feathers as hurtling ducks attract one another's attention and compete for mates.

Like the confusion of a singles' bar, the apparent chaos in the duck pond evaporates when you know the code. Learn the signals and there's no chaos at all—every movement, gesture, and call has a meaning. A drake pumps his head rhythmically up and down to lure a hen or explodes out of the water like a comet to chase a rival. He swims and turns his head to get a hen to follow him away from the crowd. Then he stretches his neck out over the water and makes several gliding passes to show interest. And so it goes, Signal A + Signal B + Signal C, clearly, methodically, until . . . doting ducks.

There's a lesson to be learned from the mating dances of ducks. For best results, our own Attention Phase signals must be clear. If at a party your "I-am-here," "I-am-female," and "I-am-friendly" cues are distinct, you will lure a man to the brink of Phase Two. Men will be drawn to you because they're programmed to respond to Attention Phase signals with approaches. This doesn't mean you'll go through all five phases, just that men will come into your personal zone of radiance.

It works the same way for men. Phase One is not the time to pursue but a time to let your silent image radiate. Show clearly who you are to the assembled women and you'll be approached. Send your *own* attention signs, not Humphrey Bogart's, Mick Jagger's, or Burt Reynolds's, because you never know what women will like. Doris Day once said she prefers ugly men because they have more sex appeal. Mia Farrow found several things attractive about Woody Allen.

The bottom line is this: you can't force yourself on anybody, but you *can* attract everyone's attention. You can't expect love at first sight, but you *can* expect attention at first sight.

Quiz

- Do total strangers ever just lock eyes and fall in "love at first sight"?
- A man approaches an unfamiliar woman who yawns before greeting him. The yawn means:
    a. She thinks he's boring.
    b. She feels ambivalent; that is, excited and fearful at the same time.
    c. She's sleepy.
- A woman smiles at a man across the hors d'oeuvre table and notices his lips tense. Is lip-clenching a positive or negative sign?
- A woman sitting next to a man on the sofa shifts her weight after he shifts and raises her glass when he raises his. Is the moment right to begin a conversation?
- If a man across from a woman aligns his upper body with hers—gives her a perfect "mirror image"—he's unconsciously inviting her to speak. True or false?
- To show a woman he'd like to get better acquainted, a man's best plan is to:
    a. Lock eye-to-eye with her for ten seconds.
    b. Wait until her gaze meets his.
    c. Sweep his line of sight several times over her field of vision.
- When a man sitting next to a woman on a bus reads his magazine a bit conspicuously—"overdoes" it, mouths the words, chuckles aloud—he's trying to "break the ice." True or false?

2

Phase Two—How to Read the Gleam in an Eye

There is no fire without some smoke.
—JOHN HEYWOOD

Look ere ye leap.
—JOHN HEYWOOD

Phase one is a bid for attention, a time when men and women volley messages about presence, gender, and safeness. Now, in Phase Two, the Recognition Phase, a man and a woman read each other to diagnose how the partner feels: Is he interested? Does she like me?

The Recognition Phase is nonverbal. No one expresses feelings in words yet. This early stage is when a person needs to know how to read gestures to gauge the partner's eagerness to get acquainted. It's very much like sonar— you bounce Attention Phase cues off someone and read the gestural echoes.

The first rule of body language is that a person cannot *not* behave. If your partner tries not to show anything, his or her body's very immobility will speak. Keeping still itself tells a tale. Most nonverbal signals are beyond conscious control anyway. And, even our reading of body language gestures is, for the most part, unconscious.

Here's an example. Everyone is aware that the pupil in the eye constricts and dilates in reaction to light and dark. But there's a psychological component to pupil size, too. Studies show that a man's pupils enlarge when he looks at photos of nude women. A woman's eyes dilate when she views nice-looking men in bathing suits, but constrict when she sees nude men. Dilation correlates with liking, and constriction with disliking.

You may think pupil size is too tiny a gesture to notice. But psychologists have discovered that we *do* see and react to another person's dilated or constricted pupils. In a classic study men shown two nearly identical photographs of a pretty young blonde consistently picked the photo with the artificially enlarged pupils as more attractive even though they could not say exactly why. Centuries ago, European women dilated their eyes with a cosmetic extract of belladonna, and today savvy card players know that dilation can tip off a good poker hand.

Most Recognition Phase signals are easier to read than pupil size. When they are read correctly, they can reveal how available a man or woman is. As a rule, women are better observers in this stage than men. Women are more sensitive to nonverbal communication from childhood on, a fact that partly explains "women's intuition." But neither men *nor* women can list, item for item, cue for cue, what leads them to decide when someone is interested or doesn't care. Therefore, a checklist of recognition cues follows.

But before we get into this candid list, before we make intangibles tangible and devise what amounts to a courting "scorecard," allow three cautions. First, no single recognition sign is 100-percent accurate. You must base your conclusion on as many clues as possible. Second, remember that courtship is intrinsically ambivalent—a potential mate will sometimes approach *and* avoid you, simultaneously—so expect mixed messages. You'll get some negative signs from every partner. And third, avoid telling the people you observe what you see. At all costs. Many of the nonverbal cues we'll be looking at are so personal, so revealing, that a partner will feel threatened knowing you're aware of them. Nobody likes to feel exposed.

Positive Signs

Eye-blink Rate. Apply the least bit of stress and our eyelids blink faster. It's out of our control. Monkeys and apes blink faster under pressure, too. We're hardly conscious of our eyelids opening or closing, let alone of our blinking rate. Like pupil size, eye-blink speed is triggered partly by psychological arousal. Psychiatric patients blink faster when they discuss topics that make them anxious.

Batting the eyelashes, of course, is a familiar flirting cue. Women brush on mascara or wear artificial lashes to embellish the blink. By disclosing anxiety a woman telegraphs that a man is arousing her. But it's a masculine as well as a feminine gesture. Both sexes blink more with partners they like. To read a man's blink signals a woman should cautiously observe his rate when he is looking at someone else, then compare it to his rate when he turns toward her.

Eyes blink faster when a person feels a hormonal jolt because sexual attraction is as stressful and disturbing as any other psychological threat. When arousal goes up, body signals fly like blackbirds out of a tree. If a person's lashes flutter when you make eye contact, assume your magnetism is strong and put a check in the plus column of your scorecard.

Gaze. Eye contact is a positive signal. On average, a stranger's eyes will rest on your face for one or two seconds before rebounding elsewhere. People have an inborn curiosity that leads them to look. Pediatrics research shows that faces naturally intrigue us. Tiny babies orient to simple drawings of facial features above all other images and show special interest in eye spots (as do monkeys reared from birth in isolation). We are programmed, as it were, to inspect faces.

But looking at a stranger's face can put us on edge. There's enough repelling force, electronic lie-detector stress tests show, that we look only briefly before our eyes bounce away. When we make visual contact, emotional arousal quickly peaks, and after one or two seconds if we don't avert our gaze we'll burst. The reason we keep our noses in magazines in cramped waiting rooms is to avoid others' eyes.

The telltale positive gaze signal is given when an unfamiliar person looks at you for longer than two seconds. Not the "bold stare," which is universally threatening and hard to take. But a slightly lingering look that just exceeds the acceptable two-second limit and then grades into a shy glance downward. When you get more than one of these three-second gazes you know there's more coming at you than curiosity. Put another checkmark in the plus column.

Mirroring. If the man sitting near a woman at a party unwittingly imitates her—crosses his legs when she does, leans back when she leans back, or headtosses with her—you can safely assume he is more than a little aware of her presence. Postural echo takes place in conversations between people who like each other. Mirroring—crossing legs the same way and so on—reveals a mutual fondness. Friends act alike, move in unison, without realizing they do so. On a sidewalk, for example, two men chatting will put a foot up on the curb and lean on their knees together like reflected images. Generally the listener mirrors the speaker.

Paralleling can happen with or without eye contact. The mirrorer might even face away. If you think someone across the table is echoing you, it's easy to test the phenomenon. Just shift forward a bit, or lean back, and see if the partner follows your lead. There may be a five- or ten-second delay, but if you notice a change of position as a result of your body shift, it's a positive sign. You deserve another plus.

Synchrony. Mirroring is a special case of behavioral "synchrony," of doing the same thing at the same time. Slow-motion film studies show that during friendly conversations listeners move their heads, shoulders, arms, and hands in time with a speaker's words. Speaker and listener "dance," as it were, to the same beat. And the more rhythmically connected a couple's movements, the warmer the rapport.

Synchrony goes deeper than conversation, however. Unfamiliar men and women may telegraph that they are on the same wavelength *before* speaking. Their synchronous body movements—tandem legcrosses, shifts, smiles, yawns, stretching gestures—may match and signify a promising kind of preverbal rapport. Just being near each other they seem to feel "good vibrations."

Body tempo, too (the overall rate of speed—fast, medium, or slow, hyperactive or hypoactive) affects a couple's potential for synchrony. A slow-moving man may not be attracted to the fast-moving, fast-speaking women at a party, and vice versa, because their rhythms don't match. When the dissonance is extreme there may be latent sentiments of hostility. You can gear up or gear down temporarily, but the elastic snap back to your own comfort range keeps the tortoises and hares apart.

Synchrony comes from an overall sensory awareness.

The more a person "feels" your presence, the greater the visible synchrony. He lifts his glass, she lifts hers; she brings her fork to her mouth, he follows suit; he clears his throat and hears an echo—it's an unwitting way to connect.

Isopraxism. But both mirroring and synchrony are parts of a still larger and rather peculiar panvertebrate ritual called isopraxism. Isopraxism means "same behavior." Just by doing the same thing—eating, drinking, preening, resting, playing, flapping, or swimming—together, two animals become allies.

When two ducks line up, dip their bills in the water, and feed at the same time, it's an unwitting sign of "friendliness." When they both preen behind their wings they strengthen the bond. In the animal world coming together often begins with an exchange of simiar behaviors.

When a man and a woman do the same thing a barely noticeable social tie germinates. A psychic closeness begins to jell as two people eat near each other in the same small deli or sit quietly reading at the same table in the public library. Even though they've never seen each other, the isopraxism works to forge a subliminal friendly, if reserved, link. It's a protoconnection, if you will. You can feel the budding closeness when you wait next to a stranger for the bus or rake leaves in a church work group. A "we" feeling develops by virtue of your acting alike.

The pull toward sameness is compelling. Isopraxism is what brings you to your feet in a theater when those around you rise to give a standing ovation. You get up whether you want to or not. And it's what starts you limping as you walk behind someone with a hip problem or pulls you off the curb with the crowd before the light changes.

Isopraxism works in courtship because anyone who does what you do is psychologically "safe." Partners will show they're on your side by imitating your gestures, postures, and activities. On a trolley car they'll mirror, synchronize, and look out the window when you do. When a woman unconsciously locks into your rhythms you know she'll talk to you when you say "Hi." Your Attention Phase signals are giving you positive echoes.

Reading Intention Cues

Equally telling Recognition Phase signals come from what are known as "intention movements." Many courting displays originate from incomplete or preparatory gestures that signal that something is *about to happen*. When your dog lifts his lips and shows you his teeth because you reached for the bone between his paws, you've witnessed an intention display. Rather than bite you there on the spot, your dog shows the beginning phase of the biting sequence to bluff you away. When your cat arches her back before attacking or fleeing from the neighbor's dog, the hump, too, is an intention posture. Her spine bows as her front end backs up against her hind end, which is moving forward. The ambivalent posture shows an intention to claw and to run at the same time.

Thanks to intention signals, people-reading can be an easy matter. When a man sitting in an easy chair puts his opened palms on the armrests and lifts his elbows, you can predict he's going to stand up. He could stay "cocked" in that position for several minutes before standing, or he could change his mind, in which case he would first lower his forearms to signal the decision. When the boss uses a similar intention cue to telegraph she's ready to leave the business meeting, the employees will imitate it and the conference will break up on cue. Here are a few courtship intention motions.

*　　*　　*

Forward Lean. When the man a woman is sitting across a table from leans his upper body toward her, even slightly, take note. Forward lean could be a sign that he'd like to move closer. The stranger barrier keeps him from actually scooting his chair nearer, so he shows the unvoiced intention and leans.

Like pupil size, forward lean is a sign that most people read unconsciously. That is, seeing the lean, a woman will "know" its meaning without realizing *why* the man—who, after all, is just sitting there reading his newspaper—seems eager to talk. Experiments show that people evaluate leaning forward in conversations as a warm, friendly cue. But well before the talking stage you'll see men and women leaning in toward one another, teetering on the brink, so to say, of the Conversation Phase. As a silent invitation, forward lean certainly merits a plus on the scorecard.

Body Alignment. The most reliable intention signal of all is aligning the upper body. Before speaking, two people will "aim" themselves, square up chest-to-chest for several minutes, as if to show that conversation is imminent. Which is to say, they show a willingness to talk before actually doing so by adopting postures that speakers use. It's like the intention to stand, which comes before the actual standing up. By squaring his torso with yours, a man indicates he's ready to speak. Give a little nod and a friendly smile and you're off to Phase Three.

Body alignment is more telling still when it's combined with another gesture, the reach-out. Here's how the combination works. Say a woman is sitting at the far corner of a table in your office cafeteria and a man sits down in the middle on the other side. She's finished eating and ready to leave but seems to reconsider at the last minute and takes a newspaper out of her briefcase. Without looking at him, she swivels her body around toward his and unfolds her *Times* on the table. No gaze, but she's aimed like a human howitzer—that's how potent her alignment and forward lean are. Now, head down, eyes on the newsprint, she lays her forearms casually over the paper and . . .

She seems to be reaching for him. But we needn't get into a deep Freudian analysis to explain the gesture. The woman is merely showing her feelings with an intention cue. Chances are she'd like to make contact but won't do so without a signal. To help tease a reaction she tosses her head and preens her hair, and . . . Recognition . . . he looks up, smiles, and a conversation begins. It's hard to ignore head-toss + body alignment + reach-out. And note, she got *him* to utter the first words, so he's the de facto aggressor.

Gaze-Crossing. But if you have a problem reading torso alignment and reaching gestures, add gaze-crossing and the amalgamated display will seem less a veiled courting message and more an engraved invitation. Sometimes people do everything but grab your sleeve to show they'd like you to say something.

When a woman is interested in a man, she would like to look at his face. That goes without saying. But unsolicited eye contact with a stranger can be heady stuff. An open gaze can brush a man back or put him on the defensive. Or—just as bad—if she glanced at his eyes the man might jump a little too eagerly at the implied invitation. What seems like such a simple matter, looking at a face, becomes a serious dilemma.

Enter the gaze-cross. Instead of giving a bald look, men and women will hedge a little and signal just the *intention* to gaze. That is, they'll invite partners to lock eye to eye, "trick" them, as it were, into making eye contact, to keep from seeming brazen.

A woman might look up from her newspaper and gaze off to her left at something irrelevant, then sweep her eyes across a man's viewfield, gaze off to her right at something equally remote, then sweep her eyes back to her paper. She cuts her line of vision back and forth across his. She won't settle her eyes on him, she'll scrupulously respect his privacy in fact, but the woman will repeat the cross until he takes the hook.

The effect is predictable. The man intuits that the woman across the table wants his attention. Her headturning creates a pressure for him to *do* something. So he yawns or scratches or head-tosses or gazes off to one side then the other, then gazes back. He peers across *her* viewfield, and their lines of sight duel like searchlights in the night sky. After contact, after the eyes meet head-on, the cross*ee* will say something to the cross*er*. Intend and it shall come to pass, the courting manual reads. Being gaze-crossed adds two points to your scorecard.

"Meaningless" Yawns and Twitches

An image comes on the TV screen. A forty-year-old man is walking toward an attractive, tousle-haired woman to introduce himself. At twenty feet, seeing him bear down, she looks away and self-consciously scratches the back of her hand. At ten feet and closing, she looks up again but quickly gazes down and yawns. At five feet, he slows his pace, smiles, dips one shoulder, looks up at her, and says hello. She drops her eyes, grabs her left wrist, smiles, looks up, tilts her head to one side, and says hello back. A courtship scene complete in four and a half seconds.

Viewing the videotape for the first time you might just ignore the scratching, the yawning, and the selfclasping. On the surface they look like meaningless gestures, unconnected to boy-meets-girl. "She scratched because she had an itch," "She yawned because she was sleepy," or, "She took her own wrist because . . . well, what difference does it make?" Seeing the tape few people pick up on the subtler messages these yawns and twitches convey. Sometimes viewers come close: "She seems nervous; she lets out the yawn as he comes nearer. . . ."

That's it exactly: the yawn *means* something. Sleepy people yawn. And we all know how contagious a yawn can be. But there's a third variety, the *social* yawn.

People yawn when they're uneasy, caught in situations of mild stress. Put a tough question to someone and he may preface his answer with a yawn. Walk directly up to a friend and she may look away and yawn before speaking. It's a natural human reaction. And like many of our nonverbal signals, yawning is primatewide. Gorillas, chimps, and baboons also yawn under stress, when impulses to approach and avoid weigh equally. Eat or play, chase or stay, join or stray—animals yawn while they make up their minds.

Conflict, it turns out, is what motivates many of our yawns and other nervous mannerisms. A woman may feel like meeting the man who always parks his car near hers, but she feels like keeping to herself, too. So momentarily at least, as they stand by their doors, she does nothing—she yawns, looks away, and scratches the back of her hand. Uncertain whether to introduce herself or be still, the woman "displaces" and does neither.

Biologists have found such displacement gestures in most higher animals. Cat owners, for instance, may wonder why the family feline always seems to stop midway in her standard greeting ritual, sit down, and lick her fur before trotting over to meow her hello and be petted. She licks herself because she gets a little too excited en route, and grooms herself—displaces—to calm down. She got a little too stimulated when the humans arrived and stopped to console herself.

Calming down is necessary in courtship because our emotions run high. In the Recognition Phase, men and women feel like coming and going at the same time. So he scratches his side, she grooms her hair, he plays with his tie, she crosses her arms, he bites his pen, and they both caress their own hands to relieve the stress.

It's fun to watch couples arriving at parties. On the front porch, after strategically maneuvering her partner close to the door, so he'll absorb the initial excited greeting, a woman reaches up and pinches the front of her neck, straightens her scarf, and tightly grips her purse. A man adjusts his belt, buttons or unbuttons his coat, turns around (averts his face from the door), and fingers an earlobe. She acts like Lily Tomlin and he acts like Johnny Carson because, if you break this little scene down to the root issues, they both feel skittish invading an occupied territory full of loudly laughing people.

Self-touching may seem irrelevant, but it's really quite functional. Stimulating your own skin helps take attention away from whatever's bothering you. This is why we fondle touch stones and worry beads or caress a blanket's satin binding. Self-manipulation is the body's way of bringing energy back to "center," as it were. People displace because it helps to control anxiety.

Watch for displacement gestures and you can—metaphorically—take a partner's pulse. These "meaningless" behaviors make reliable recognition signals because they show your presence has an arousing effect. It's psychological rather than sexual arousal at this stage. When the unfamiliar man or woman across from you yawns, head-tosses, or adjusts a cuff after meeting your eyes you know your Attention Phase signals have been received.

Ask yourself if she would be primping her hair quite so briskly or if he would be picking his fingernails quite so absorbedly at home alone watching TV. If the answer is no, then chances are you're the reason.

The Courtship Smile

Unlike the unwitting body signals we've seen up to now, smiling can be manipulated and controlled. We can grin on purpose. Parents tell children to beam happy faces at the camera, and from years of urging we develop an automatic push-button smile. But Mom and Dad don't care *how* a child smiles—the lip corners just have to turn up. So the grin still has a certain unaffected, spontaneous meaning to disclose in courtship.

When an unfamiliar man or woman looks at you and smiles, take it as a positive sign, but not necessarily deserving of a plus. After all, smiling is the standard friendly greeting in all cultures. Conversely, not being smiled at is usually a bad omen, but not always. Some people just may be so nervous around you their faces seize up before a smile can get off the ground: the lips start to flex, then quiver, then tighten, and finally slam shut before the smile has a chance to show.

A smile has so many nuances it's hard to pin down one easy meaning. Grinning has a deep-rooted ambivalence built into it. Smiling evolved from the primate "fear grin," a protective facial expression monkeys and apes give in situations of high anxiety and extreme threat. By "grimacing," pulling the lip corners back and showing the teeth, a chimp shows submissiveness. The fear grin says "I'm harmless" and keeps more powerful animals from attacking. Biologists say our smile works on the same principle and carries two meanings, fear and liking.

Our friendly grin is not the simple pleasure signal we take it for. Think how you might smile when meeting Johnny Carson for the first time—probably more than he would smile back. Which is to say, the smile is tied more to fear, status, and anxiety than to happiness. So any way you look at it, smiling is a complex courting signal.

If a woman gives a "simple" smile, that is, if she smiles with her lips closed, chances are it's the courtesy grin she gives all strangers. In courtship simple smiles don't reveal much one way or the other. But if she beams an "upper" smile—shows her top teeth—the greeting could be a bit more than routine. An upper smile from a stranger across a room merits a plus on the scorecard. But if a man stands pinching the plastic stem of his champagne glass and a woman flashes him an open smile—both rows of teeth show (as well as the glistening gums in the awesome Jimmy Carter supersmile that seems to stretch beyond the confines of the face)—it could be an unqualified invitation to "come get sociable." Rate the supersmile three points.

Negative Signals

Don't be dismayed if you receive a sprinkle of less-than-positive signals in the Recognition Phase. Ironically, getting a negative signal or two is good, because it helps you know who's seriously courting and who's just out for a fling. If a person gives only come-on signals, you may be dealing with a Casanova or a career vamp. On the other hand, if *all* you see are aversive courting signals you might want to locate your zone of radiance elsewhere.

Most negative signals stem from innate protective responses. All the stranger-anxiety cues a baby gives off are for defense and self-preservation. Infants automatically turn away from suddenly approaching objects so they won't get hit, even though they've not yet learned that a basketball caroming off the head is painful. The body is prepared, it seems, with vigilant gestures.

And because the signals are innate they're difficult to

fake. Aversive cues leak from the best con artists, even ooze from the pores of insurance men, to let the careful observer know their true feelings. Few parents bother to influence a child's unfriendliness. Mom rarely says "Put a little more feeling into that tongue-show" or "Wipe those compressed lips off your face." When you see a negative courting signal you know it's authentic.

Seeing a "cold shoulder," a "freeze" or any other aversive cue, most men and women will feel demoralized and stop courting. But a few will press on and refuse to take no for an answer. Some intrepid men won't respond to a subtle hint, or even a blatant one—they will court no matter what comes at them, like the character Benjamin in *The Graduate*. Persistence can pay. Anyone sensing reluctance is better off testing matters before quitting entirely.

To test an "unfriendly" reaction, first make a hypothesis about why it occurred. Your best working assumption is "It's not my fault." Give a person the benefit of the doubt. Repeat, "It's not my fault," and go ahead. But approach from a different angle, try another room, or wait until the targeted person sits down. Then, if you get a second minus signal, give it a rest. Maybe the man or woman is just in a sour mood. The signals are reliably negative, but you can't really know what's causing them. So wait twenty minutes and try again. If the person is still a gargoyle of grimness, then quit. No use being a fool about it. The point is not to react immediately to body signals, as most people do, and rule a person out because you feel hurt. Negative signals often mean a person is taking a protective—not necessarily an unfriendly—posture.

Be scientific. Test the signals.

Cold Shoulder. Say a woman is standing across an hors d'oeuvre table from a distinguished-looking, bearded man. She's sixty, he's fifty-five, and they both came to this church ice-breaker for single seniors at the urging of friends.

After some careful maneuvering she finally catches his attention and their eyes meet. But he quickly breaks contact and slowly turns his left side toward her and dips another chip into the guacamole. An ominous sign. He aims his left shoulder at her and doesn't gaze back. She's just been shut down by a classic negative courting gesture. He's given her the cold shoulder.

Threatened by a barking dog or a stumbling panhandler, the body's automatic reaction is to turn away. Both the head and the body instinctively avert to the side away from the danger. It's known as "cut-off." Cut-off is partly protective and partly an "ignore-it-till-it-goes-away" or an "out-of-sight-out-of-mind" response. The man above reacted to the woman's frontal approach and unwittingly turned away. If she had used a less threatening *sideward* approach he might have been more sociable. After waiting a few minutes her best next move would be to come at him from *his* side of the table before establishing eye contact. From that position she would be psychologically less upsetting and easier for him to deal with.

No Reaction. The absence of any courting signal—nothing positive, nothing negative, just a matter-of-fact reaction as you pass by (the typical waiting-line, bus-depot, airport nonperson treatment)—is more daunting than outright hostility. In boy-meets-girl no reaction is the most damaging signal of all. When you stand near someone, smile, align your torso, and give the permissible one-or-two-second gaze, and all you get back is casual notice, a blank face, tight lips, and narrow eyes—the eyes brush over your body as if it were no more interesting than a filing cabinet; there's no spark, no hormonal twinge—put down a minus sign on your courting scorecard.

Men especially have a hard time reading no reaction. Many misread the cue. Sometimes a man assumes all is well if a woman barely tolerates his presence. He's so enchanted by her gender cues—the pretty face and figure turn his head—that he entirely tunes out her behavior. It's known as "Pygmalionism": falling in love with statues. There's the celebrated case of a young Russian man, for example, who was arrested for paying moonlight visits to the statue of a nymph, and that of a Parisian gardener who fell in love with a statue of Venus. Some men court whether a woman moves or not.

Freezing. Freezing resembles the no-reaction response, but the motive differs. Fear, not indifference, makes a person "play dead." Temporary immobility is the last word in shyness. A panmammalian signal, motionlessness comes from the death-feigning posture we call "playing possum." Nature programs an animal to freeze its movements so predators will lose interest and call off the attack.

Boy-meets-girl can be so frightening to some people that they just go rigid near good-looking partners. A woman might pull her forearms tightly into her abdomen or clamp her hands together on her skirt like a wax-museum figure. And she'll stay paralyzed—only her eyes will move—until the man she likes goes away. It's hardly indifference, and the submissive stillness distinguishes freezing from no reaction.

As a Recognition Phase cue the freeze by itself is neutral. You can't tell from immobility whether a man or woman likes you or if he or she is just intimidated by your being nearby. Freezing is a common reaction many of us have around celebrities whose status makes us feel inferior. Combine a smile ("I like you") with the shy freeze posture ("I won't resist") and the courting message is positive. But add a tongue-show or tensed lips and it's as if the person is playing possum with you—"I'll pretend I'm dead until you go away." An obvious minus.

Tensed Lips. Men and women can hide a lot of feelings, but they can't keep tension from showing in their lips.

Even tiny distresses can trigger tightness and strain in the intricate musculature around the mouth. A person's lips will thin and roll inward as they contract. The greater the anxiety, the greater the tenseness, until the lips actually curl in and disappear.

Part of what leads us to ask someone, "What's wrong?" is lip compression. Tight lips are an innate signal of displeasure. Babies clench their lips when they're angered or upset by strangers. Men compress their lips in arguments; women clench when they shake their heads side to side in disagreement or disbelief. It's a natural sign of aversion and a negative social cue.

She doesn't seem too friendly, the man thinks, because every time he sweeps his gaze across her she unwittingly tightens her lips and turns her head away. These gestures show he's on thin ice. And indeed the woman *doesn't* like being close to him, so she'll "tongue-show" (protrude her tongue so it just shows between her lips) or she'll bite or lick her tensed lips—which is to say, her mouth will tell it like it is: "I don't like you there; move back."

But when a person smiles *and* compresses the lips at the same time, you get a Johnny Carson-type "ambivalent" grin. Ironically, "mixed" or ambivalent smiles are positive courting signs. The closed, lips-rolled-in smile shows the proper mix of "I like you" and "I'm a little timid around you, too." Score all tensed-lips signs with a minus, but give the ambivalent smile a plus.

Arm-crossing. Popular books on body language interpret arm-crossing over the chest as a "barrier" gesture, as a sign warning "Come no closer." But you see crossed-arms signals all the time in flirting couples. "Barrier," therefore, is inaccurate. The arm-cross is better viewed as a self-clasping gesture. As we've seen, people hang onto themselves in anxious settings. Like Jack Benny, they cross arms to console themselves. So-called "barrier" gestures can be positive signs that show your presence affects a partner. The cross shows they're not taking you for granted.

Tandem arm-crossing, that is, when you and the person near you both cross, is an affirmative sign, too. So is crossing combined with smiling. But with a tongue-show or tensed lips, crossed arms can connote negative feelings. The most nay-saying crossed-arms display of all, though, is what I call the "Richard Nixon." The "RN" combines folded arms with an evasive torso. It's the "shifty" pose we've seen Mr. Nixon use—arms folded low on his chest, face and body turned away—in his dealings with those he felt uncomfortable with.

The RN position is one of several basic "squirm" postures, which combine anxiety with a reined-in desire to flee. Mr. Nixon tacked on a politician's hair-trigger grin, making the pose all the more ambiguous and "tricky," but most people's faces, when they do the RN, are expressionless ("deadpan") or obviously troubled—you see frowns, pouts, lip-clenches, and lip-bites spastically going on all at once. Courting anyone who is locked into the RN position is a little like wooing a post. The posture says the person is in no mood to court back. Wait until a man or woman comes out of this posture before making a move.

Postural Mismatch. The last unpromising Recognition Phase cue is postural incongruity. The greater the mismatch between your own head, arm, hand, foot, and trunk positioning and that of someone sitting or standing near you, the greater the psychic gulf. Dissonance in body carriage is a sign of social distance.

Unlikeness shows unrelatedness. Take seating positions. If you're sitting cross-legged on the floor and a man strolls over and sits down, carefully note his posture. If he sits, say, six feet away, on the floor, cross-legged, give yourself a plus. Even though he may not glance over at you the mirroring is a positive sign. But if he sits six feet away in a chair, and stretches his legs out away from you, chances are he's less interested. Even though in each case you're both facing forward, that is, you're neither turned toward each other nor turned away, the match is promising and the mismatch unpromising. Unless he changes his position—turns his upper body toward yours or gets down on the floor within five minutes—put a minus on the scorecard.

The Summing Up

Most people don't carry pads and pencils with them to parties. The average person courts without strategy and leaves it all to chance. Which is OK if you are, as they say, "lucky at love."

But watch these "fortunate" popular people operate and you'll see that they're less bewitching than they are sharp observers. They beam out Attention Phase cues and pick up all the echoing blips and beeps on their minds' powerful radar. They read the crowd intuitively and mix with those who come in strongest on their receiving screens. The lucky person's antenna is always on.

Observing Recognition Phase signs gives you a strong edge in courtship. Anytime your mental scorecard tallies up to plus three—the positives and negatives balance at three or more—you know you're dealing with someone who likes you. After twenty minutes tally up the score, then take a positive person with you into the Conversation Phase. If he or she finds you attractive *before* the speaking stage you won't be as prone to strike out. Which is easy to do, as we'll see, because speech is the cruelest phase.

If someone registers ten, you've reached courtship's version of the ionosphere: "love at first sight." Most books on love and marriage dismiss the instant-love phenomenon out of hand. Contrary to popular opinion, the experts will tell you, love at first sight is only an illusion, a fraud. No one falls in love suddenly on Sunday, October 30, 1983, at 4:02 *P.M.*

But the "experts" are wrong. Love at first sight does exist. It is rare, but enough couples have described the experience—chance eye contact followed by an intuitive flash of recognition across a crowded room, just before Cupid releases his arrow—that its reality cannot be denied. Love at first sight happens in the Recognition Phase when a great number of positive cues spark back and forth in one searing pulse, and a man and woman fuse in *amoris extremis* after five seconds. After meeting Ronald Reagan for the first time, Nancy said, "I knew right away."

Love at first sight, though, is truly chance because so many plus signs must fly at the same time. It's like two coveys of quail exploding at each other out of different bushes simultaneously. And preconditions need to be met. Faces, body types, age, clothing, and so on must match the partners' ideals. Then comes the initial gaze—with dilated pupils, batting lashes, raised shoulders, canted heads, synchronous self-clasping, matched tempo, postural echo, body alignment, head-tossing, and shy smiling, all of which grade into "tortured looks" or great pumpkin grins—love at first sight. Highly irregular, but it happens.

"Attract at first sight" is the normal Recognition Phase plan. Men and women often attract one another immediately, but there's not the mutual outpouring of cues that instantly pulls them head over heels into the vortex of each other's admiration. The cues tend to be understated and strewn out over a period longer than five seconds.

It may take three weeks for recognition signals to work. Take one young woman's story. She was nineteen, he was forty-four. Ironically, it happened in 1944. She had a long sweep of silky hair, large, wideset eyes, full lips, a small, straight nose, and every attractive signal available to the human face. His face, etched with authority-connoting wrinkles, had "character"; he had a gravelly voice and a Pepsodent toothpaste smile. He was famous; she was cute. A perfect match.

In their first scene together, her head and hands shook visibly. She averted her face, kept her chin lowered almost to her chest, and gazed up at him—the coy look. "No flirting," she wrote later, but they did a lot of kidding around, laughing, and smiling. Each was gentle with the other. She described him as "shy." They must have mirrored and synchronized easily as they ate, acted, played, and practiced together isopraxically, because both knew they were heading for trouble: he was already married. People talked. Anyone could see the signals.

But they liked each other—a lot. Too many recognition cues had changed hands. And after three weeks, it happened. She described it as an imperceptible shift toward closeness. "I don't know how it happened," she wrote in her autobiography. One day he walked into her dressing room and threw down the gauntlet. He stood behind her, they joked, he leaned forward, cupped her chin, kissed her. Then Bogart took out a worn pack of matches and asked "Slim" to write her number on it. She did. The rest is history.

Of course, the famous courtship of Humphrey Bogart and Lauren Bacall had by this time progressed to the verbal stage, Phase Three. Nonverbal communication can take a couple only so far.

Quiz

- The best way to impress a stranger to whom you are attracted is to simply walk up and say so, straight out. True or false?
- Men should memorize four or five "formula" opening lines to make small talk easier at parties. True or false?
- A sure sign of attraction is when a woman
    a. Points her index finger.
    b. Rolls her hand palm up.
    c. Makes a series of palm-down sweeps.
- In the mating game, what you *say* is less important than the fact that you say *something*. Yes or no?
- From the very start, a man should call a woman by her first name. However, a woman who uses a man's first name too early will seem forward. True or false?
- It's easy to know when a man is flirting with a woman by the way he speaks because:
    a. His voice is pitched higher.
    b. He seems excited and a bit "childlike."
    c. He keeps "checking" your reaction with his eyes.
    d. All of the above.
- In courtship the adage "Never speak until you have something to say" is true. True or false?

3

Phase Three—
What to Say
and How to Say It

*Other parts of the body assist the speaker, but the
hands speak themselves.*

—*QUINTILIAN*

The almighty word. Courtship won't advance to the touching stage without conversation. Things need saying before
men and women lay on hands. Speech is a rite of passage
in courtship in every society. Making it to the speaking
stage, to dialogue, is a quantum leap ahead in the
progression. Even when ethnic backgrounds differ and a
man and woman can barely understand each other's mother
tongue, they still talk, because a wooing tone sounds as
sweet in Mandarin Chinese as it does in Parisian French.
In the Conversation Phase, words are as necessary for *how*
they're said as for the meaning they carry.

Indeed, much of what we say during courtship carries
little "meaning" in the ordinary sense. "Hello!" "How
are you?" "Great day, huh?" "What's happening?" and
so on are versions of *grooming talk*. Just as many animals

show affection when they groom a mate's fur, we show friendliness with words, with comments that don't mean much more than "I notice you."

We trade "contact" sounds just to let people know we appreciate their presence. In courtship, especially, speech may be "meaningless," that is, content free. The meaning of "Hey, big boy" or "O-o-o-o-o-*wee*, baby" is rather like the "peep-peep-peeping" of just-hatched chicks, which means "I'm here."

But don't think all the words uttered in this stage are trivial. The Conversation Phase would not be the difficult screening test it is if ooo-wee's and skoo-by-doo's were all we needed to say. Men and women disclose a lot about themselves when they speak. Intelligence, education, social background, likes, and dislikes all go on the line. As soon as you open your mouth you stand . . . exposed.

Exposure is why it's often so difficult to get into the Conversation Phase. People sense they're likely to be put through a tough cross-examination when they speak to someone to whom they're attracted. And indeed, Phase Three can be a long-winded trial. Many couples never get through; others may take years. The hazards of speaking can make breaking the ice the scariest step in courtship.

Many men and women are afraid to say anything. They hang back in the shadows. You see them at parties and singles' bars, the "wallhuggers," the people who neither sit in nor walk through the middle of rooms. But even those who find mixing easy often have problems sweet-talking their way through the silk-fine screens of Phase Three. Many a courtship ends with a whimper in dialogue or stagnates in a conversational holding pattern.

What's in a Word?

What makes speaking such an ordeal? Why do couples spend weeks, months, and sometimes years in the word stage before proceeding any further down Cupid's path? The reason is that conversation puts physical closeness to a severe test. Consider what a man and woman must actually do when they speak. In a head-to-head conversation, they must stand closer than three feet, often as near as eighteen inches, measured nose to nose. And the pair must *stay* close for the duration, for from three to five minutes for the average party chat. What's more, both must look repeatedly at the other's face.

Talk about pressure. Chatting with an attractive man or woman can be embarrassing because conversation locks you into a closeness that's unnatural. There's no biological precedent for the sustained nearness or the lengthy eye contact speaking puts us into. No other animal hooks up face to face in courtship quite the way we do. Our speech-mandated eye-to-eye contact is unprecedented in nature. What other animal must gaze into a potential mate's eyes for weeks before giving the first touch?

Only human beings go through such prolonged eye contact in the mating game. Standing only eighteen inches away you see all the facial signals up close—the hair, the skin's smoothness, and its wrinkles, pouches, and pits, the teeth, the whites of the eyes—where impact is extreme. You smell the breath, hear the subtlest voice tones, and feel the body heat. Personality resonates clearly at speaking distance, because it is virtually cheek by jowl.

And you synch into a complicated, finely tuned pattern of gaze. He looks and she looks away. He gazes and she gazes down. The listener looks, the speaker averts; the speaker glances, the listener averts—time spent eye to eye is often but a small part of the total conversation time. American women fixate longer on eyes than men do, statistically, but neither sex gazes continuously without gazing away. Looking away is necessary at close range to help participants relax. Eye to eye, our heartbeat rate increases because direct gaze arouses. A glance away for only three seconds can bring the rate down as much as ten to fifteen beats per minute. So we alternate our gaze in order to shed the stress.

When men and women speak, they communicate on two levels at once. The conversation itself, the words you could record in a written transcript, go on at an intellectual level, on a plane of thought. Spoken dialogue is a true meeting of *minds*, because words are processed in the brain's higher speech centers. But at the same time, down lower, beneath the witty repartee, men and women also have a sexually loaded *emotional* experience. When they come face to face with each other's masculine or feminine signals they may feel a hormonal rush. Gender cues are processed in older, deeper "courtship centers" while the dialogue runs. A couple can talk about nuclear physics or Malibu—it doesn't matter—and flirt at the same time.

As you become fluent in love's nonverbal language you will notice a certain sexual tension in nearly all relations between men and women. Note that most conversations are a bit flirtatious even though serious sexual contact probably will never occur. Courtship is such a bedrock issue in human nature that its metaphors show whenever a man and woman talk. You can tell a caller's sex just by listening to the answerer's tone of voice. For example, a female caller will evoke higher pitched replies from men as well as women. Face to face, you'll note that familiarity *and* avoidance rituals work, side by side, to balance our desire to draw people close against our fear of letting them come *too* close. When a woman talks to a man, for instance, she may feel a tension in her gaze as she wonders "Am I looking at him too long or not long enough?" She's talking on one level and taking sexual inventory on another.

As necessary as talk is in boy-meets-girl, starting a conversation is never easy. It's not that talking itself is difficult. After all, even three-year-olds speak. And it's not as if the stranger barrier keeps us quiet. We talk to unfamiliar gas-station attendants and waitresses all the time. But these people stand in familiar *roles* to us. Clerk-customer has its own easy rules. With someone you're attracted to, on the other hand, the "potential-lover" role doesn't make for easy conversation.

Speaking to a possible sexual partner for the first time can be agonizing because you put yourself in jeopardy. Addressing someone, you implicitly obligate that person to respond. In effect, you burden the man or woman with a covert message: "Talk to me." But putting yourself forward is not the only stress that comes with saying something. What if the person ignores you or thinks you're presumptuous or doesn't like your opening line? Speaking doesn't just put you on the line, it hangs you way over the edge.

How to Start a Conversation

Opening Lines

"Hi [smiles]. I'd like to talk with you to see if we have something in common [moves closer and bears down]. You look like a very interesting person [grins]. Tell you what . . . how about if we just talk for . . . [looks at watch] five minutes, and if you want me to leave after that I will [brows lift like birds of prey]."

But of course. The man who said that just got through reading a how-to manual, because his up-front, straight-ahead, no-holds-barred opening line is one of a host of "direct" approaches suggested in the recent avalanche of how-to-pick-up books for singles.

His brassy opening line might work. But so would, "Got a match?" Social animals that we are, people respond to almost any comment because it's the polite thing to do. But in courtship a person wants more than a courteous response; he wants dialogue. And no stock opening line or magic formula exists to make a woman converse against her will.

What's more, the up-front approach is not really on the up-and-up. It comes at you like a verbal ramrod, pushy, like a radio commercial. And note how the speaker puts all responsibility for ending the dialogue after five minutes in *your* lap. He casts you in a potential spoiler's role if you turn him down. And what's really direct about telling a woman she's "interesting-looking," when you both know it's only a formula to make sexual headway?

Contrived "direct" approaches and cute opening lines—"I can tell you're left-handed because the right side of your smile is higher"—can actually damage rapport. Understand the root nature of speech, its deep psychology, and even conversations in artificial settings like singles' bars will be easier and relatively free of strain.

Grooming Talk. Many people think they should keep their mouths shut until they can say something thoughtful. As far back as the 1700s John Witherspoon advised, "Never rise to speak till you have something to say." A good idea overall, but not in courtship. "Empty" grooming talk is a valuable courting tool. Having nothing to say might be reason not to speak out at a conference of atomic scientists, but not at a party. At parties, vocal contact is more important than sounding intelligent.

You may think a man needs to hear something more than, "I like your jacket," and that a woman needs something more substantial than, "Great party," before they'll speak to you. But it's not so. The personal interest such comments reveal is worth more than any "brilliant" statement, such as, "Yes, and what do you think about the War of the Roses?" Meaning is mostly beside the point in an opening statement. The human voice has a special drawing quality of its own.

Infants automatically orient to the sound of a person's

voice. Human vocal tones, studies show, strum precisely the right chords in a baby's brain. Voices can calm, soothe, and hypnotize. A wailing infant will quiet down if you hold it up near your face and speak in a soft, droning tone for a couple of minutes. The voice has a beat and a tune, a musical effect that works apart from the ideas conveyed. The sound alone can mesmerize.

Still, the hardest thing in courtship is saying the first words. But once you're relieved of having to show brilliance and wit, speaking is easier. The opening line is merely a device to make contact. "Hi," "How are the nachos?" "Nice party"—such simple utterances suffice to show your interest and break a stranger's protective bubble of reserve. The show of friendship, human to human, is merely that.

It's smart strategy to say a brief hello to people at a party as soon as you can. Make an effort to say a few words right away—there's no need to start a lengthy conversation. Once you create a vocal link, talking is easier all evening. Your early, "What's cooking?" to the man peeking into the oven at the bacon-wrapped scallops, or the early, "Which way to the bathroom?" makes it easier for a partner to say something to you later on. The only hard part is getting past the first words.

Networking. No one trusts "the stranger in our midst." Strangers are so distressing that every society has found ways to classify outsiders and type them into familiar categories. Even the cultural anthropologist who travels to study another society's customs is pigeonholed. This odd foreigner normally becomes a special-class "uncle" or "aunt," a "brother" or "sister," or a make-believe grandparent—that is, an honorary relative with family links to important people in the tribe. Threatening as a stranger, the anthropologist, safely connected in the familial network, becomes kin.

"Fictive kinship" is part of a larger need to know where we stand vis-à-vis others in a hierarchy. "How do we relate, you and I, in this group?" is a universal human concern. It's the first thing people ask you at, say, Bob and Sue's party: "How do you know Bob and Sue?" Your reply helps answer the deeper, *un*asked question: "How do you relate to me?" By finding a social link through Bob and Sue you connect, feel more secure and subliminally "safer" through the tie. It's the "any-friend-of-Bob's-is-a-friend-of-mine" formula.

In courtship it's helpful to establish a primary link with unfamiliar people *before* speaking. Ask Sue who that woman in the corner is—"Oh, you mean Debbie? She's a philosophy major at Vassar"—and: Primal Link. "Hi. Sue was telling me you're at Vassar studying Plato." Because you're both tied to Sue, Debbie's root feeling is that you're OK.

The main idea is, Don't be a stranger. You may have noticed that women rarely go stag to restaurants, parties, or bars. The obvious reason is that men will descend on a lone woman like buzzards. But it goes deeper than predators and prey. Women seem to understand a basic truth of human nature, that a "loner" is psychologically less desirable than a member of a group.

Loners are universally untouchable and feared. So sociable is the human animal that anyone without connections seems almost subhuman. A loner feels something is basically wrong with him. He feels like a loser, as though he doesn't have what it takes. Both the loner himself and the socially valuable people with partners who sit in judgment of this potential outcast unwittingly think along these lines. In a singles' bar few women will talk to an unconnected man, no matter how romantic the lone-wolf image of Marlon Brando or James Dean.

Outside of one's circle of friends anybody feels a bit alienated. But you needn't bring the forlorn image with you to a singles' bar or a party. Go with a friend. That's good advice for men *and* women—go with someone you know, because you'll seem more sociable and therefore much easier to talk to. Alone, you can't show your social cues, your smiles, head-tosses and shoulder-shrugs. But don't stay tethered to your comrade. Sometimes it's easier for a person to speak to you when you're by yourself. Just make sure people know you're not a potentially dangerous hermit.

One of the best ways to talk to a stranger is to draw that person into an existing conversation. Invite the nice-looking man across the table to participate in the dialogue you already have going with your friend. Signal you're accessible with the position of your body. Instead of huddling confidentially inward during your chat, and sealing others out, sit or stand with your body turned *outward*. That way he knows he can join in. An added benefit of this ploy is that while you're talking to your friend your gaze can linger on unfamiliar faces in the crowd. As long as they know part of your attention is invested elsewhere, the glances will seem less threatening.

Food. Few grasp the deep connections between speaking and food. All over the world people who eat together talk together. It's part of a primordial "feeding-time" psychology. Eating is powerfully sociable. And chewing a bite of food makes a person seem more human, more vulnerable as it were, and less likely to snap at you. People become more convivial, more expansive, and better natured as their stomachs fill. Their blood-sugar levels rise. Most barriers to conversation come down when you eat near someone, an effect you can experience in a jet-liner when meals are served. Even reserved people come socially alive when food arrives on their tray tables. It's hard to eat together in total silence.

The single most sociable thing you can do in any culture is share food. So even when people won't take the nachos you offer—even though it's universally bad form to refuse food gifts—they'll appreciate the gesture. By proferring food your status invariably upgrades to "friend."

A prime courting tactic, therefore, is to order fingerfood—an appetizer, shrimp-stuffed artichoke with hollandaise sauce, or mixed nuts. At a table crowded with unfamiliar men and women your food's presence will make conversation easier. The group will unwittingly shift into the more sociable feeding mode. You will seem like a safer, more trustworthy human being *just by eating*. And everyone around will notice you more, because food is impossible to ignore.

Shared Focus. Anytime you approach an unfamiliar person and ask a question or say the word "you," the addressee is likely to become mildly defensive. It's natural to bristle a bit. A personal question puts a subtle demand on you, because it obligates you to respond. The word "you" is slightly forward, as well, a little too personal coming from a total stranger.

Rather than meeting someone head-on with an opening line, it's better to be indirect. The best strategy is to avoid any direct reference to "you personally" and refer instead to something you both see, feel, hear, or smell, that is, to your "shared focus." Comment on the crab dip.

Shared-focus remarks are intrinsically oblique, in fact, triangular. You're A, your partner is B, and the classical music, the rose in the white marble vase, and the aromatic pipe tobacco you both smell are all C. The idea is to think about C and come up with a simple declarative sentence. That's your opening line.

Saying, "Mozart—great!" or, "I smell Cherry Blend," lets a partner know you're willing to make contact, without obligating a reply. You reveal the immediate focus of your attention, the music or the aroma, and invite the person near you to share it. There's no compulsion and no threat, only a free invitation. A model of obliqueness: A and B come together through C.

Shared focus is the active ingredient in the conversation piece. You might feel uncomfortable talking to the man standing beside you, but put a cockatoo on his shoulder and there's no problem. Your new calculator watch or your silver matchbox works the same way. Shared focus— you give anybody who wants to speak to you an easy way to do it by setting up the oblique center of attention.

Embellishing. Another way to invite conversation is to embellish an ordinary, everyday activity. Overdoing is a subtle way to draw comment. You can tell when a woman in a restaurant wants attention by the way she looks at her watch. Instead of a quick glance, she'll overextend her arm, reach it all the way out front, then dramatically bring the wristwatch back to her face, tilt her head, and read the dial. This exaggerated gesture gives anyone nearby permission to ask, "What time is it?"

Notice how a man sitting near an attractive woman puts more energy into eating his Big Mac burger. He'll turn it this way and that, inspect it from all angles, lean way over to take a bite, wipe his mouth with too-forceful rubbings of the napkin, and give off more than the usual number of head-tosses to embellish the eating ritual. And the near-clinical examination of the hamburger invites her to join in with something like, "Here's some extra catsup. . . ."

Embellishing is an effective tactic. People will unravel your body's tale and speak—if they want to. If not, at least you haven't put yourself in jeopardy. It's a soft-sell way to telegraph your wish to be spoken to.

When you see an embellished routine, don't hesitate to join in. The person wants you to say something. Ask yourself if she would be writing in her notebook quite so energetically at home alone. Would she lean her head down quite that close to the paper, bite her pen, look up quite that high, wrinkle her brow quite that thoughtfully, dive down to write another line quite that manically, or erase a word with that much energy? If not, she's inviting you to share her focus. A simple "Is that a poem?" could be enough to ignite a courting dialogue.

Proximity. Finally, just being physically close to a man or a woman can be enough to jump-start a conversation. As we've seen, being near someone is stressful, arousing, annoying, or pleasing—in a word, *disquieting*. Unless the reasons for the closeness are already obvious, a person will need to explain why he's there. Nobody sitting next to you on a bus needs to justify the proximity, of course. But a man and a woman waiting under the same chandelier in a deserted hotel lobby at six in the morning will speak, a bit eagerly, in fact, to reassure each other they mean no harm. Alone together and physically close, two people are extra friendly, extra polite, to put each other at ease.

The proximity effect can work nicely as a courting device. At a party a man standing by himself on the sidelines is an easy target. All a woman need do is calmly walk over, stand about six feet away, turn so her body faces whatever his faces (note the implicit "we" feeling that comes with facing the same way), and sip her drink. She neither has to make eye contact nor say anything—the proximity and her calmness will speak for themselves. Within sixty seconds, as pressure builds to explain the unusual closeness, he will turn and say something.

The basis of this meeting technique is extremely covert. You might think walking to within six feet of a person and standing there is, well, a bit blunt. "He'll know I'm up to something," you might suppose. But our minds don't work that way. The move will confuse him; he'll puzzle about why you're standing there and not saying anything. And a person's reasoning is so topsy-turvy in the nether-lands of stranger psychology that *he'll* feel somehow at fault. Ironically, he will need to explain *his* existence to *you*.

All the techniques so far discussed work because they're based on studies of how real people in natural settings—in office buildings, shopping malls, parks, and so on—actually open conversations. Overall, the pattern is this: unless an opening line is invited, unless it flows from a shared focus or embellishment or networking, it seems forced. There's always a way to make speech contact just as long as what you say streams from a natural source.

People suspect anybody who drops comments on them out of the blue. I won't forget one sad episode that took place in the back of an overheated city bus. A young woman sat down and took off her bulky down jacket. Just then a handsome young man asked her, out of the wild blue, "Why are you taking your jacket off?" It struck me as an odd question, because the temperature inside wasn't just warm, it was tropical. He was only trying to make contact, but the woman pulled her brows into a puzzled crease and said, "It's hot in here. . . ." To which he replied, shaken by her narrow-eyed look, "Well . . . I think . . . [mumble, long pause] . . ." She cut him off and began to read her book. How much better it would have gone if he'd just asked, on the basis of the shared-focus principle, "I wonder why it's so hot in here?"

The Gestures of Courtship Dialogue

With the opening line you enter the labyrinthine Conversation Phase proper. Once you've spoken, or cleverly finagled your partner into breaking the ice, you're in for a lengthy stretch of dialogue. Now comes courtship's most trying time, a period of data collecting and verbal dueling, a subtle "trench warfare" of words.

"That man that hath a tongue," Shakespeare wrote, "is

no man, if with his tongue he cannot win a woman."
Forgive Shakespeare's chauvinism: reverse the sexes and
his observation still holds. All a man or a woman needs to
do to win in Phase Three is be truthful. No amount of
fabrication or deceit will be more attractive than the bona
fide you revealed in words. The real man or woman is
more interesting than any fictional character you can create.

Trust one who, after doing fieldwork in a hundred little
places where the singles play, knows the difference between a courting conversation and a line. No one cares if
you've traveled the Orient or run with the bulls in Spain.
Tell someone you've touched Mick Jagger if it makes you
feel good, but that fact won't help you squeeze through the
conversation screen. The best way to proceed is to disclose
who you actually are, reveal your true feelings, and show
an interest in your partner.

A lie detector is a child's toy compared to the body's
own techniques of telegraphing distortions and lies. Try
presenting a false image and you just won't seem . . .
legitimate. The deceptions will show. And even if you do
con your way into what Gay Talese so poetically calls the
"downy billows," at some point you'll be found out. I've
listened in on countless courting conversations, and the
most effective dialogue is between people who are being
themselves.

But enough about what to say. How do people behave in
the Conversation Phase? How do you know if the person
you're talking world politics with truly likes you? What
signals tell you it's time to move on to the Touching
Phase? What can you do to show the man or woman you
like that you care—without showing too much?

All this boils down once again to nonverbal cues. *How* a
person says something is as important as what he or she
says. The Conversation Phase is perhaps even more gesture laden than Phases One and Two. You can easily tell

which couples in a restaurant are making progress. Watch for the following.

Palm-Showing. Courting couples bring each other in with gestures. Instead of sitting like stonefaced judges behind a bench, they smile, raise their eyebrows, nod their heads, and, perhaps most telling of all, they show their palms. One of the best courting gestures is the "palm rotation."

By rotating your palm to an upward position and extending the uplifted hand toward your partner, you bring that person in. Your gesture makes whatever you say seem more personal. The upturned palm makes a speaker's words feel warmer and friendlier.

You can test the gesture. First ask a friend, "How's it going?" with your arms relaxed, hanging loosely by your sides. Not moving your hands makes the phrase rather noncommittal. Then say it again, but this time bring your right forearm up (keep your upper arm in against your ribcage) and aim it at the addressee. Now, open your hand and turn up your palm. That's the palm rotation, used worldwide as an affable cue. To make it more personal still, swing your right upper arm forward, as if you were going to shake hands, and keep the palm rolled upward. You've just sent a strong message of friendliness.

Courting couples use open, palm-up gestures almost exclusively when they talk. They show the palms, without thinking, because doing so telegraphs gentleness. Trace the gesture's origins and you'll find it's the hand position taken in the shoulder-shrug display. Once again, we have an exchange of aggression-denying cues. Palm-showing is another way for men and women to take it easy on one another.

Look around a restaurant at the couples who aren't using palm rotations, and you'll see they're also not courting. That woman over on the right . . . she's leaning toward the man she's with (a good sign), but her index finger is stiff as steel and it's aimed right at his chest like a knife. An assertive sign. He's listening with his lips compressed and his hands set rigidly on his hips. No, definitely not courtship . . . and listen . . . they're arguing about some real estate deal. Not a fun lunch.

Or that couple on the left—definitely married—they're having a relaxed chat, leaning in on each other across the linen, but there are no speaking gestures at all. Both have their elbows on the table and their hands clasped under their chins in the classic posture of satiation. They're blissfully stuffed and comfortably on good terms. A courting couple would keep on rotating their palms to reduce the psychic distance, even after they got the check.

Potent Focus. Actively courting men and women bring a visible intensity to their first few conversations. They square their upper bodies, hold them parallel, and lean in toward each other across a table. It's as if they're trying to leave an impression. If the fire alarm were to sound, the waiter would have to pry them apart, so exclusive is their orientation. No touching yet, but the magnetic posturing shows it's just around the corner.

Look over at that booth under the hanging fern. High-power wooing, because the man leans forward and holds his opened hand up by his ear. That "walling-off" gesture helps make what he says seem even more exclusive, for his date only, and he keeps bringing the opened palm down from his ear, up, and down again, to lock her into his conversation. And she's absorbed. Note the rapt posture, as if she's afraid to turn her head a millimeter either way for fear of showing anything less than whole-hearted attention.

Leaning forward shows you're interested in your partner. The lean also magnifies your overall impact, the good as well as the bad. If you're coming across well, leaning forward will make you seem even better. But if you're not doing well, leaning ahead will make you seem worse. You'll know which it is, because when your performance starts going downhill the partner will let you know by leaning away or turning the head to one side—the squirms and cut-offs will tell you to back up. Or maybe you're just talking too much. Remember to take turns.

The conversation itself will be potent in a winning courtship dialogue. There will be hardly any "dead air." People who really like each other have little trouble talking. Just the opposite—they find it hard to stop. You'll notice a lot of heavy eye contact as the couple does more than their share of visual checking to monitor and play to each other's reaction cues. And you'll hear laughing as they agree eagerly about everything—never again will two people get along quite like this. "Do you like linguini?" "No, but I love spaghetti." "Oh, yeah? That's my brother's favorite food." "Wow, I don't have any brothers, but I have a sister who lives in Italy." "That's amazing—my favorite actress is Italian." And so it goes.

Heed the signs. If your own conversation sputters fitfully along, if he has dead eyes, if she never leans forward—accept what these gestures tell you. Enjoy the food and don't feel like a failure. Analyze what's happening and learn a lesson. Predominantly negative signs at a meal, the most sociable of human rituals, tell you *not* to move ahead in the progression. It wouldn't be worth the pain of trying to get along the morning after.

Submissiveness. When a man and woman are interested in each other they'll exchange signs of submission and vulnerability in the Conversation Phase. Beware of anyone who doesn't show you something meek. No matter how persuasive the words, don't begin letting down barriers until a man or woman gives you a few childlike cues.

Without them, chances are the partner is less than truly attracted.

Listen to tone of voice, pitch, and loudness. When men talk to each other they use louder, deeper voices to convey their manly authority. But man to woman, the conversational tones are quieter, lighter, and higher. Men speak softly around women they like.

A woman, too, is more soft-spoken—she turns down the volume and raises the pitch—with men she likes. It's the voice she uses with babies, small children, and fuzzy pets. Both men and women use the softer "caring" voice around partners who stimulate their cuddle response.

You can tell you've pushed the right buttons in a conversation when your partner gives off signs of vulnerability. Women will tilt their heads sideward, pitch and roll their shoulders, and sometimes even bounce up and down slightly like excited children. Yea-saying women often sit or stand facing you with one shoulder held noticeably higher than the other. A woman's face will tip forward a bit and she'll glance up at you from under her eyebrows. All her signals will invite you closer.

Men present basically the same signs, but are more inhibited about it. Their movements will seem stiffer and a little reined in. Nevertheless, you will detect a childish bearing in an amorous man early in Phase Three. One typical posture men use when speaking with women they like is the placing of their hands through the knees. A man will lean forward in his chair, rest his forearms on his knees, reach his arms forward, and clasp his hands. Sitting that way, he'll look like a little boy, a blushing third-grader stretching out toward his pretty teacher.

Intention to Touch. In successful courtships the Conversation Phase slowly grades into physical contact. But before actually touching you your partner may telegraph an intention to do so.

Chatting with a woman beside him, a man will casually reach his hand over onto her chair's armrest and leave it there, inches away from her thigh. Or a woman standing at a patio bar may take hold of her icy Mai Tai and position the glass and her hand inches away from a man's elbow. You know it's an intention to touch because your partner stays in the closer-than-normal position for minutes on end. This close to you—within eighteen inches, definitely penetrating your personal zone—your partner telegraphs a readiness to touch.

The Right Touch

Touching is what talking is about. At least it is in courtship, because the whole idea of the Conversation Phase is to draw men and women together physically. After you talk to someone, you either feel like touching or the courtship ends.

The Conversation Phase can be arduous and drawn out. Partners don't often measure up to each other's expectations. At some point in a casual chat you may see a couple polarize and repel each other. But not *everyone* gets screened out.

Take Rosie and Charlie. It was wartime and they'd just met. German soldiers had come to the Dark Continent, causing them to flee. Charlie knew there was only one way out: the river. And there was only one boat: the *African Queen*.

It was tough going at first. But they talked and talked and gradually got acquainted. Rosie didn't like Charlie drinking all that gin, so she dumped his stash overboard the morning after the night he drank too much and called her a skinny old maid. They argued, but they kept talking, on and on. They adjusted, and things improved.

Charlie shaved, cleaned himself up. Rosie relaxed her

steellike spine and loosened her shoulders. Their voices softened. You could sense new feelings—affection.

Rosie went for a swim in the tropical waters and couldn't climb back on the *African Queen*. So Charlie took her hand and pulled her onboard: the First Touch. Their hands and arms brushed as they both held the tiller and shot the rapids below the German fortress: the Second Touch.

All that intensive conversation and "accidental" touching over a period of days drew them closer. You could feel affection turning to love. When the *Queen* went over that impossible waterfall you knew romance was inevitable. If Rosie and Charlie survived they'd *have* to make love.

Indeed. And when they were safe in gentle waters they jumped for joy and hugged (the First Embrace), and he kissed her (the First Kiss). And the best part of the film was Hepburn's wide-eyed shock and Bogart's subsequent frowning, pained look—overdone but still true to life. They'd gotten to know each other better than either had known.

And who can forget that fantastic line of Hepburn's after the first serious caress: "Dear, what is your first name?" Courtship—nothing has changed.

Quiz

- When a woman at a picnic "accidentally" touches a man's shoulder as she reaches for her iced tea, it means she's interested. True or false?
- When a man reaches out and administers the first touch—pats a woman's wrist or playfully takes her elbow in his hand—he'll know she's *truly* touchable if she:
    a. Tips her head over to one side.
    b. Raises her shoulders.
    c. Touches him back.
- Locked in a first embrace, you find yourself being gently "rocked" and patted on the back. Which of the two cues is better?
- You know the hug you're getting is serious when:
    a. You embrace from the side and your hips touch.
    b. You glance at each other and giggle.
    c. You both experience a sudden "hush."
- A man is about to deliver the first kiss and his date compresses her lips—tightens and rolls them inward. Should he kiss her on the mouth or change course and kiss her cheek?
- Sitting together on the living room couch, a woman knows things are getting serious when her date:
    a. Shifts into a "parental" mode and slows his pace.
    b. Nuzzles her cheek with his nose.
    c. Gives her his best *en face* gaze.

4

Phase Four—
The Language of Touch

Most decide by "the touch," that is, the feel . . .
—ANDREW URE

Jane Wyman and Regis Toomey kidded for 185 seconds in the 1940 movie *You're in the Army Now*. A lengthy labile touch by any standard. Still, a trifle compared to Debbie Luray and Jim Schuyler's marathon five-and-a-half-*day* kiss on February 14–19, 1980, in Florida. But even that world record pales in the face of James Whale's feat, 4,049 girls kissed in eight hours. Never have so few kissed so many or so long.

Once a couple arrives at Phase Four, after all the talking (with Murphy's Law ensuring that whatever *can* go wrong *will)* they're close indeed to the final, Lovemaking Phase. During the Touch Phase, couples shift out of the Speech Phase into a tactile mode. They lay on hands, transcend the logic of talk, and communicate in a more candid, persuasive medium.

The skin is our largest and oldest sense organ. Touch therefore has a deeper meaning than speech. Something we touch seems more concrete than whatever we only see, hear, or smell. Touch convinces our brain beyond a doubt that a thing is *real*.

In courtship, only the ancient language of touch can convince and reassure us that the ultimate closeness, sexual intercourse, will be OK. So, before making love, we "handle" each other.

But not just any touch signal will serve. The best tactile signals—the kiss, the caress, the snuggle, and so on—come from the parent-child bond. We touch lovers the way we touch babies. Every sweet gesture a mother makes toward an infant and every cue a child gives back have been transferred, *as is*, into courtship. What better way to convince a partner than to stroke her face or pet his hand? Rub a man's nose and a childish twinkle registers in his eye. Pat a woman on her bottom and you'll usually evoke a grin.

Maternal touch signals permeate animal courtship, too. Enamored elephants caress and intertwine their trunks; chimpanzees hug, kiss, and pat; whales nuzzle; baboons groom; possums lick. Gentle touching, stroking, and licking tame the beast, as it were—bring out the harmless infant and stimulate infant-care attitudes in the adult animal at the same time.

When a man or woman touches our nearly hairless, and therefore very sensitive, body, that person has our complete attention. Touch is a narrower, more-exclusive form of communication than speech, that is, more one-on-one. And the meaning of a tactile cue is more emotionally charged. A soft, stroking movement of fingertips on the nape of the neck, for instance, bypasses the thinking parts of the brain and cuts directly through to feelings. What's more, the touchee will either like or dislike the signal immediately, because touching evokes a clear "yes-or-no" reaction.

With the first touch, courtship begins to move faster. Indeed, it moves *too* fast, many couples report. The tactile mode exerts a kind of tidal pull toward completion. The shift from vision and hearing to touch drops courtship to a more-primal brain level, and control shifts downward to primitive neural centers whose mute authority verges on the dictatorial. With the hands laid on, courtship gets *out* of hand.

The First Touch

True sexual arousal begins with the first touch. But how do couples manage the initial contact? In very public places, like restaurants or theaters, men and women sometimes defer the first touch and handle a "body extension" instead. A body extension can be a purse, a glove, a notebook, a briefcase, a book bag, an umbrella—anything a person wears, holds, or keeps nearby to supplement the body's own natural endowments.

Body extensions boost our powers. But possessions are more than inanimate objects. Umbrellas, purses, and gloves also partake of our personality. We "rub off" on our belongings. Touching a man's pocket calculator is almost like touching his wrist. It's the same in all cultures. A man's axe or a woman's net bag in effect becomes a part of that person's body. Touch the axe and you touch the man. In courtship, touching body extensions is a hedge because the owner can't feel the contact. Nevertheless, he'll react as if you'd handled the skin itself. And the reaction is your clue.

See what kind of effect just reaching across your colleague's desk and picking up his stapler can have. If he's interested to begin with, your running your fingertips along the chromium base will affect him as strongly as if you'd just fondled his hand.

Or better yet, watch the popular "jewelry-handling" technique many men use in bars. As if gripped by an overwhelming interest in a woman's watch, a man will span his index finger and thumb over her wristband like a caliper and say something profound about digital timepieces. Touching pens, pencils, sleeves, cigarette cases, lighters—it's all the same in courtship—hedged first touches.

Then come playful games of keepaway. At a party a man will put a woman's lighter in his shirt pocket with a smile and say, jokingly, "Thanks." Next thing you know, they're wrestling—first touch. He's got the lighter in his hand, and she's prying his fingers loose, a grin on her face. Radical "courtship keepaway" ends with a couple locked in a variety of wrestling holds. Suddenly pressed together, they dissolve in embarrassed laughter. They separate, feeling a bit sheepish and confused.

Extreme forms of courtship keepaway are mostly a teen-age thing. As people get past adolescence, hormonal exuberance wanes, and first touches become less obvious. But you'll still see playful tickling, grabbing, and soft poking after the age of twenty. A woman will wind into a high giggle and jab her fingers into a man's side at a party to tickle him. A man will kiddingly poke the shoulder of a woman he's been flirting with at a dinner party. A man and woman will read each other's palms across a table. It's all very light and "unserious," of course.

Some first touches are more emotional than playful. A couple will be talking, tightly focused on each other, and the listener will exclaim, *"No!"* or, "You're *kidding!"* or, *"Oh yes!"*—put a lot of feeling into it—then look away, extend an open hand, and touch the speaker as if to say, "I'll use this time of shared high emotion to feel your skin and we'll both pretend it's not serious." The laughter seems to express just that.

From the giggling you might assume first touches are never serious. Laughter masks the sexual meaning, but touching is strong stuff indeed, neural TNT. And while the brain's emotion centers jump for joy, the more-reasonable gray matter of the neocortex tries to cover up the true significance of first contact with slurries of disclaiming words. Along with laughter you'll hear a lot of fast talking as the hand comes sheepishly away again.

Many first touches are "accidental." A woman reaches over a man's shoulder for a napkin, extends herself a wee bit too far, and presses her fingertips into his shoulder blade to keep her balance. Or a man shakes another man's hand in a crowd while his thighs gently brush against a seated woman's knees. Both seem to ignore the touching, but deep down they know it's a crucial test.

Reaction-testing is the prime reason for any first touch. Skin-on-skin contact is like a stethoscope over a heart; it gives you an accurate courtship reading. Overall, people respond warmly to brief touches with the hand on a sexually neutral body part. A light, one-second touch on the back of a hand, a wrist, or a forearm when you're talking can lead a person to feel significantly closer to you, and at the same time let you gauge the hormonal pulse.

In the first touch, avoid a partner's head. People naturally flinch when you reach a hand toward their eyes. You won't get an accurate reading if you touch the head. And necks, chests, hips, and so on are too sexually loaded. A person will think you're taking liberties. Touch the back of your partner's hand, or his arm or shoulder from two to three seconds to validate the mood.

With your hand resting on the back of a partner's wrist, what do you look for? If your partner freezes, faces away, tenses his lips, or bites them, if he involuntarily withdraws his hand or stiffens his upper body—*back off*. Such aversive cues can mean the partner is not yet ready to be touched. Wait five minutes and try again to be sure, but chances are the message will only be repeated—"I'm not ready for you to touch me."

If, on the other hand, your partner raises her shoulders, tilts her head to the side, places her toes in, or gazes briefly into your eyes and then glances downward, she's telling you, "I accept." The best message of all, though, is being touched back. When you both lay on hands, large-caliber tactile signals are sure to follow.

The First Embrace

Never grab unless the "grabee" is up for grabs. That's the unwritten rule of the Touch Phase. But if a partner approves warmly of your first touch you may soon be ready for the next step, hugging.

The courtship embrace has instinctual roots. Babies are programmed to clasp and cling. The Moro reflex, functional from birth to four months, is the human version of an ancient, primate-wide "hugging" pattern. In times of danger infant monkeys and apes automatically cling to the mother's fur. They know, without being taught, how to hang on. Grasping is instinctive in humans, too; a newborn baby is able to hang, unaided, from a clothesline.

This primate hug has been pressed without substantial modification into our courtship. The adult hug shows parental affection and psychologically reassures the hugee. To many of us, indeed, the hug signal is as important as lovemaking. Being held produces a primordial sense of security and comfort. Studies show that substantially more women than men crave being hugged, a fact that explains the sex appeal of large-girthed, hugable teddy-bear types like Italian tenor Luciano Pavarotti and TV star Ed Asner. Many women value the affectionate and reassuring qualities of hugging more than sex itself.

Some women make love to be hugged, and some men hug to make love. It often seems as though men and women are wholly different species. But on average, both males and females enjoy courtship hugging. For not only does the embrace soothe and express warmth, it also excites and gives a couple their first taste of whole-body closeness.

Generally the first embrace comes soon after the first touch. Opening brushes and pats quickly seem tame, and the body wants more. A man will feel a hormonal pull standing next to the partner he's been sparring with all evening, and in an emotional gush he might hook a hand around her waist, or cup the fleshy part of her upper arm, and lock her into a side-by-side hug. As their hips press together, he will give two or three rhythmic squeezes and pull her tightly toward his body.

Side hugs are playful. Every signal up to now, in fact, has been light, frisky, and mischievous. The joking, frivolous qualities of early touching are signs that a commitment has not yet been made. Partners can still back out gracefully because the laughter and frolic provide an escape hatch. No one wants to commit prematurely.

But then something comes over a relationship that can only be described as a "hush." The couple joins in their first frontal embrace, and from then on courtship virtually stampedes. When a man and woman wrap their arms around each other, press their torsos together and lock pelvic girdles—not the family-style hug, where close relatives lean forward to keep their pelvises from touching, and self-consciously pat one another on the back—you know they're moving toward Phase Five.

The serious full-frontal hug is courtship's first private display. Up to now all the signals have been traded in public. But you'll find most leisurely embraces exchanged in hallways, bedrooms, or outside in the intimate shadows under the silvery moon.

If your scientific curiosity gets the better of you, and you can observe without getting caught, note what happens in this liminal "hushed period." You're witnessing a ma-

jor shifting of psychic gears. With the true embrace, courtship switches into cryptoreverse warpdrive. The speed of
the interaction slows, as if the couple were being lifted by
mysterious updrafts. It goes like this:

Their smiles fade and their faces become deadpan. Mouths
open slightly, eyelids drop into a half-closed, sleepy position,
and, in extreme cases, partners will raise *and* lower their
eyebrows (that is, activate both sets of competing musculature at the same time) in what Charles Darwin called the
look of "grief." When attraction is irresistible, you'll see
forehead creases tangle as if at cross-purposes—the same
"tortured" look Bogart gave Hepburn in *The African Queen*.
A man and woman locked in the frontal embrace will
suddenly synch into a very leisurely tempo, the very slowed
speed they may use later just before making love.

The First Kiss

Locked into a frontal embrace the couple is nearer to Phase
Five than either might imagine. Sensing their seriousness,
they move away from others. Around the world, privacy in
sexual matters is the rule. Where automobiles or empty
rooms are not available, there's always the "bush tryst."
It's a pancultural thing: people everywhere meet in the
bushes to hug and exchange arousal signals if there's no
better cover. If a couple embraces frontally in public,
onlookers will heed their seriousness and "ignore" them.
Note that when a man and woman hug in the middle of a
busy sidewalk, pedestrians give them a wide berth and turn
their heads away as if an invisible zone of privacy bil-
lowed around the entwined couple.

You'll feel some embarassment at watching couples at
this stage, because the privacy tells you they're on a fast
track to sexual intimacy. But it's worth overcoming the
natural urge to hide your eyes. Few behavior patterns are

quite as fascinating as the move from hugging to kissing.

First you'll usually notice a gentle, side-to-side rocking, a subtle swaying motion. That parental signal helps reassure the partner, makes the closeness seem OK. And you'll see the couple square up their faces, eye to eye, nose to nose, their gazes locked together, their heads only six inches apart.

This eye-to-eye gaze, or the *en face* position, is another mother-child remnant. Peering into his face from this intimate distance, the partner's eyes will seem to merge into a single image. Already sealed off from others in the frontal embrace, and spatially removed as well, the partners both hold visual images of one giant eye in a corona of skin, and their exclusiveness is complete—the partner is all that exists in the universe. "It's just you and me, Baby," is more than a line now; it's a sensory truth.

Ever so slowly, the couple's heads will loom closer and closer, like docking spacecraft. Three inches away and closing, their faces will roll several degrees right or left, in synchrony, so the noses will clear. And the lips begin a cautious link-up. The pair seals together in the first kiss.

The kiss signal plays a pivotal role in courtship's stream of behavior. Lip contact shows that this couple is moving ahead in the progression. But they're too stiff, too inhibited yet to be a mated pair. Note how they still must choreograph their kissing exchanges.

When the man turns toward her and sees a closed-mouth smile, he moves in and kisses. But if she gives him an open-mouth smile, shows her teeth, neither moves forward. The open smile works here as a kiss-nullifying signal.

Anthropologist Adam Kendon has decoded the pattern. The woman's "dreamy-face" expression seems to give the man permission to kiss longer. First they face each other and the man rubs the tip of his nose on her nose. It's the legendary Eskimo kiss. And whenever they rub noses she gives him the "dreamy face" as she lifts her eyebrows and parts her lips in depleted ecstasy. When he sees that seductive expression he approaches and they go into a longer, drawn-out kiss.

It's interesting how the woman seems to control the man with the signals she gives. To end the kiss she pulls back her head, protrudes her tongue, swivels her face away, and looks off behind her shoulder. To deflect an approach she turns her head slightly when he moves in, dodges, and shows him an open smile. It's all closely synchronized. Even tiny cues mean the difference between success and failure. If the man were to try to override her open smile's "brake," she would no doubt consider him far too pushy. So he rubs noses to evoke the "dreamy face" and gets a long kiss by pushing the right buttons.

The kiss is a primordial courting signal. Actually, kissing is older than humanity itself. Many mammals "kiss" before mating as a way of stimulating a partner's maternal instincts. Dolphins nibble, cats give playful bites, dogs lick faces or nuzzle flanks, and chimps press lips in their courtship.

Our kiss originates from a mammal-wide sucking reflex. Lips evolved to give our mouth an airtight seal around a nipple. Sucking, the puckering as well as the rhythmic lip-and-tongue motions, is instinctive. So is a baby's habit of turning toward your finger when you gently stroke his cheek. This, the rooting reflex, drops out of an infant's repertoire at four months. But fragments remain. Rooting explains why we nuzzle our faces against a lover's face.

Kissing stimulates both parentlike and childlike feelings in us. Every society uses some form of kiss or nuzzle gesture in courtship. Not only do you find lip-to-lip contact, but lip-to-tongue, tongue-to-tongue, nose-to-nose, and cheek-to-cheek signals, as well as an exotic assortment of biting and face-rubbing, in the world's cultures. Just as adults feel compelled to press their noses against a baby's buttery face, so lovers touch faces to reassure each other they mean no harm.

In Phase Four words also carry a strong parent-child flavor. Voices become softer, higher in pitch, and slower in tempo. The voice is that a mother or father uses when picking up a small child. There's a breathy, purring, drawling quality in a loving tone, and the vocabulary speaks for itself: "baby," "kitten," "sweetie," "chick," "sugar daddy," "little lady," "cutie," "dollie," "mama," "old man," "honeybunch," "darling," and so on. The "littleness" that many pet names convey, the diminutive connotation, is found in many languages in the speech of lovers, from Russian to Spanish to Marathi.

In the Valentine's Day messages newspapers publish, linguistic cuteness runs to extremes: "Poosie loves her Billiam" (a diminutive of William, no doubt); "I love you, Sugarbumps"; "I love Funny Bunny"; "I wuvva wuvva you" (duplication of syllables is a favorite children's game); "You're my Cupcake"; "Chocolate-Pudding Eyes"; "Baby Cuddles"; "BB Bear wuvvs Kewpie Doll"; and so on. And lovers' nicknames also emphasize childishness: Zippy, Clarkie, Misty, Pumpkin, Melba Toast, Peanut (note the harmlessness suggested in edibles), Pooh, Pooter Bear (bears, with their rounded features and fuzziness, are always in vogue), Pooper Dooper, June Bug, Snookie Pie, Little Gorfee, Boo-Boo Face, Bunky, Sweet Cheeks, Craigipoo, Jimmy Poo, and Boobly Boo carry the "be-my-baby" theme to its syrupy conclusion.

And We Just Couldn't Stop. . . .

By now, with serious kissing well underway, the couple is on the road to sexual intimacy, want it or not. A person may have serious doubts and think the whole thing is wrong—conscience never speaks louder than it may now—

but nature will let no reasoned cry interfere with reproduction. Stopping courtship at this point is like trying to
stop an arrow after you've released the bowstring.

The pace picks up again. Faces nuzzle and hands play
on bodies in a fast dance. Having shifted totally into the
tactile mode, courting's most powerful channel, it's too
late to ask, "Can't we just be friends?"

The Touch Phase starts out innocently enough: "accidental" contact or touching a nonsexual body part with the
fingertips. (Some view the entire human skin as an erogenous zone, so "nonsexual" may be a misnomer.) You
touch, feel the right pulse, and move on in turn to the side
hug, the frontal embrace, the *en face* gaze, and the slow
kiss.

After the lingering mouth contact, courtship goes on
automatic pilot. From now on, tactile cues seesaw back
and forth so smoothly it's difficult to know who, the man
or the woman, actually takes the lead. In truth leadership
shifts back and forth as each one moves as far as the
partner's signals allow.

"You think too much," Bogart's spirit scolded in *Play
It Again, Sam*. Sitting close by Woody Allen's left shoulder,
advising him how to proceed, move for move, with Diane
Keaton, who was sitting to Woody's right on the sofa,
Bogart urged him on: "Kiss her before she gets out of
position."

But as we all can't have an acknowledged expert to
counsel us in Phase Four, and because partners—even
those who talk your ear off about everything else—never
just *tell* you what to do next, you must read the emitted
cues. Eyes close, breathing deepens, faces flush, and knees
go weak. It's time to sit down. Touching becomes "heavy"
as hands move across bare skin in ever-larger arcs. Women
cling more, men caress more, and hands move toward the
sensitive genital tissues.

By now the neocortex is switched off entirely as tactile

cues send a gong-ringing message to the brain's pleasure centers. Picture a couple poised on the brink of sexual contact, genitals just millimeters away, and mentally freeze the frame. Considering the hundreds of courting signals exchanged to get to this point, let's just savor the moment. . . .

Quiz

- "We can keep it casual" is often wishful thinking, especially after a couple has intercourse. True or false?
- You can easily spot a "mated pair" because:
  a. They give off fewer courtship signs.
  b. They take the distance separating them for granted and touch at will.
  c. They stand closer than unmated pairs.
- Your date's grip tightens noticeably as you turn your head to pull out of a kiss that seems too long. Could failure to release you be an early warning sign of impending "date rape"? Yes or no?
- On the cusp of courtship's primal Lovemaking Phase, some men claim they "lose control and can't stop." To help change a man's mind a woman should:
  a. Reason with him first, and if he doesn't stop, plead.
  b. Suddenly scream in his ear loud enough to evoke a visible startle.
  c. Give him an unambiguous physical message his brain's pain center will grasp.
- In the middle of fervent lovemaking a woman's partner "spaces out" and seems removed. He's probably lost interest in her. True or false?

5

Phase Five— Love Signals

Love looks not with the eyes, but with the mind.
                                        —SHAKESPEARE

With genital-to-genital contact we arrive at courtship's most intense, most pleasurable stage. Also its shortest. Phase Five (which excludes foreplay) rarely lasts for more than three minutes. That's how long the average man keeps going until climax and its deflating aftermath bring the love act to a close.

More signals shuttle between partners during this final courting period than in any previous stage. Indeed, Phase Five communication is so "hot and heavy" many couples find themselves not just physically close but psychically cemented. So many primal messages going back and forth can bring a couple closer than either partner had bargained for.

"Primal" is an understatement. Consider one Love Phase signal, the pelvic thrust. Just as soon as penis and vagina meet, thrusting begins. The genitals make up-and-down, side-to-side, and circular movements against one another.

Pelvic thrusts have deep evolutionary roots in the brain's reptilian core. Just as giant tortoises instinctively thrust when they mate, no human being needs to learn from *The Joy of Sex* how to thrust. Since thrusting motions are as basic as crawling, sex manuals devote most of their teachings not to thrusting, per se, but to slowing it down to prolong the pleasure.

If you think in a detached way about the whole thing, what two more unlikely body parts could men and women bring together? Knowing that we would hardly submit to such an absurd juxtaposition without some major reward, Mother Nature coated our genital organs with a highly sensitive veneer of ''sexual skin.'' Gentle touching of the specialized nerve endings will send quivers of pleasure right to the brain's pleasure centers. If the sexual skin were on our little toes instead, we would blissfully rub our digits together.

Although embracing, nuzzling, and rubbing sexual skins are gratifying in themselves, most men and women experience an ecstatic final pleasure in Phase Five, an orgasm. Orgasm is part of our prize for making love. The warm, pulsing, glowing, rushing ''fireworks'' display in our brain is there to signal that we did indeed have a good time ''doing it.''

Orgasm's Roman-candle effect—the giving and receiving of extreme pleasure—is one of many signals that help convince couples to stay together, if not forever, at least for months at a time. During the period of close togetherness, lovers tend to be faithful. They feel less desire for other lovers and feel cheated if the partner makes love on the side. Such is nature's plan to provide for the continuation of the species.

Every signal of the sexual act reinforces the exclusiveness of the newly formed love bond. The full-body contact imprints a strong tactile image of warmth and softness that sticks in the memory after the lovemaking stops. The skin's sensual musky odors register in primordial centers of the ancient "smell brain." Even the sexual posture itself—face to face, chest to chest, extremely intimate—helps couples to fuse a bond.

If courtship cues pull us in, love signals hang us up. Keeping a relationship casual—"just friends"—after Phase Five is often difficult. Ask any married man or woman who is locked into a nerve-jangling affair if the intentions were serious from the start. Our form of making love is more expressive, more signal laden, than any other form of human expression.

Most animals mate for extremely brief periods by human standards, often for a matter of only seconds. Shaw's jird, a desert rodent, holds the world's copulation record: 224 times in two hours. That's thirty seconds per.

But our own much-longer period of lovemaking—fifteen to thirty minutes if you count foreplay—gives us time to exchange a hundred tender caresses. These intimate signals can release such an outpouring of parental and dependency feelings that by climax we truly become each other's babies and cling together.

What Is Love?

Reduced to its simplest terms, love is one part attachment and one part lust. That, of course, is a cavalier oversimplification, but look closely at any doting couple and you'll see them exchange both parental and erotic signals.

Signals of Lust

Erotic signals well up out of the most archaic part of our neural anatomy, the reptilian core. Lust—eros, raw desire, "the urge"—is wired into certain primitive ganglia in the base of the brain. From there, lust drives our sexuality like a turbine. You can see passion in a man and woman who, embracing and locked *en face*, unwittingly drop their mouths open. The parted lips show they're so overcome by emotion they've lost control of their jaw muscles.

Open any *Playboy* or *Playgirl* magazine and you'll see half-opened mouths beckoning at you from the nude models' faces. The photos look all that much "sexier," because the brain mistakenly assumes that you yourself caused the mouths to drop. That's why pictures of naked men and women beaming big grins just don't seem erotic. Smiling shows they're still in control.

Another lust signal is half-closed eyelids. You see droopy lids on people as they bring their faces together to kiss. Like parted lips, drooped lids show that control has downshifted to the erotic pleasure centers. Which is why both men and women are attracted to "bedroom eyes." Rudolph Valentino and Jean Harlow knew what lazy lids signified.

Lust is the "cardiac-respiratory" aspect of romance. In 1943 Joseph Folsom, a social psychologist, wrote that the love feeling is visceral, a profound and exhilarating sensation in the chest area. Maybe so, but cardiac love signals— flushed skin, deep breathing, pounding heart, tensed hands and feet, quivering legs, weak knees, sighs, moans, and groans—are only half the picture. These purely physical reactions are necessary but not sufficient by themselves. For one thing lust doesn't always focus correctly on human partners. Animals can become the objects of free-floating desire, as can melons, shoes, throbbing exhaust pipes, and leather goods. They're all on record in the psychiatric literature. In one classic case a man became sexually excited by safety pins. . . . There's more to love than heavy breathing.

Attachment Signals

Deep feelings of parentlike *attachment*—the root emotions of "broodcare"—blend with basic lust in Cupid's mixing bowl. Sexual desire combines in equal parts with nurturing to make true love life's greatest pleasure. Most of us want above all to live with a sexually attractive, nurturing person.

How do you know if a partner is just "using" you or if he is truly attached? The signals are almost too obvious to name. Nevertheless, these signals are often missed, and the attached person—who, after Phase Five, has been hooked, dragooned, and utterly *hung up* on you, and shows it in every gesture—still must put the obvious fact into words. Most of us don't understand what's happening until a partner finally says, "I love you."

But the *unspoken* signals are legion. Anyone totally infatuated with you will give a certain diagnostic grin that's undeniably genuine. The attachment grin is like no other smile. Cheek muscles contract violently and pull the lip corners so high on the face they quiver from the strain. It's an uncontrollable smile that shows pure joy. There's no sarcasm, ambivalence, or humor in that beaming look, just love.

Anyone who has fallen "in attachment" will want to sit or stand close, just to be near you, and if possible, touch you unrelentingly. After Phase Five, a smitten person will give you lingering looks, sigh a lot, play down your faults, want only you, and think about you constantly when you're gone. So strong is the loving feeling when it first hits that a mate often won't feel like eating, sleeping, or working.

You can see the same attachment cues in animal courtship. When Toto, a home-raised female gorilla, first met Gargantua, a male ape who traveled with a circus, she stared in surprise, barked in rage, and threw back in his face the stalk of celery he offered. But at home with the Hoyt family, Toto "fell in love" two or three days each month with the chauffeur, the gardener, or the butler. In a reversal of the classic *King Kong* plot, Toto pursued a man, followed him, and sat and stared at him with lovesick eyes. The Hoyts had to come between Toto and her loves, to keep the amorous ape from laying her hands on the men and drawing them to her hairy bosom.

Few human beings have any difficulty recognizing lovesick eyes. They're a worldwide attachment signal. Actually it's not so much what the eyes do—they're fully open and staring right at you—as it is the position of the eyebrows and the set of the lower jaw. The eyebrows just barely rise, as if the lifting takes every last ounce of the lovelorn's depleted energy reserves. And the face goes slack; the lower jaw drops open but the lips remain closed, so that the bottom half of the face looks longer than usual (the "long face"). Because the lovesick person sits without appearing to breathe (the lungs remain in exhale position), he or she seems caught in a terminal sigh.

We can also empathize with the transmitted emotion. Lovesickness is a mild form of depression, a feeling of loss. It's what homesick children experience the first time they're away from their family overnight. Separated from Mom and Dad, they hang their heads, bow their spines, unfocus their eyes, seem listless, and sigh. H. F. Harlow's infant rhesus monkeys curled themselves up in the same vacant-eyed, defeated postures when he took them away from their mothers.

Seeing either manic or depressive signs in someone you've recently slept with is firm evidence that his or her feelings have gone beyond lust. It's a wrap.

Swinging Sex

In a bedrock sense, then, love is attachment *and* lust.
When couples break up—when they move through the
phases in reverse—the heartache, the sorrow, and pain
come from love's attachment side. Nobody cries about lost
sex. The horny get desperate, not depressed.

Just how wedded lust and attachment truly are can be
seen in our failed attempts to keep them separate. Take
organized "swinging," a 1960s phenomenon that rode
into America on the wave of the sexual revolution. The
guiding lights in San Francisco and Big Sur reasoned that
men and women could short-circuit courtship and *make*
love, as it were, *without* love.

Swinger courtship is brief. Couples are prescreened before a party starts to keep out dangerous psychotics. Everyone is safe because names, telephone numbers, and medical
test results are on record in the host's files. Men and
women do all they can *not* to get acquainted. First names
only, a quick martini, a nod, a wink, and a single sentence:
"Would you like to go upstairs?" Then a swift move to
heavy petting and a savored Phase Five, done in a variety
of impersonal, acrobatic positions. Keep it physical.

But swinging, mate-swapping, and so on don't go quite
according to plan. Somewhere in the orgy room things get
personal. Cliques form, jealousies fester, and before long
John and Marsha are giving each other lovesick looks
behind the sofa, because courtship takes couples down the
love path despite themselves.

Even Hugh Hefner, a playboy's playboy, a man with
more sexual degrees of freedom, perhaps, than any other
man in America, searched for true happiness outside the
harem, with one playmate in particular, Barbie Benton.

It's not easy to fool Mother Nature—sooner or later the courtship signals get to you.

Love's Danger Signals

"Love looks not with the eyes, but with the mind," Shakespeare wrote. As usual, Shakespeare should be read in the literal as well as the poetic sense. Indeed, the brain is our largest sexual organ, because that's where all our courting programs are filed.

Unfortunately, courtship has a dark side. Sometimes it's hard to know where delight ends and distress begins, because pleasure and pain connect in the brain. In certain deeper grottos of our reptilian core, positive and negative images are lashed so closely together that they overlap and set one another off in odd ways. Our programs for mating and mayhem sometimes get hopelessly tangled, like the strands of a cupboard mop.

So we're heir to a Pandora's box of twisted practices, such as sadomasochism and sexual killing. It's not our fault that the buttocks teem with nerves from the larger erotic nerve net or that pathways for anger intersect with genital pathways in the brain. That dominance and submission and sex are all wired together is a fact of nature. That's why we have musical groups like the Sex Pistols and movies like *Dressed to Kill*.

Anyone who courts should keep an eye out for danger signals. Women especially need to monitor a partner's aggressive tendencies. Too many men can get perilously out of control.

Take what is known as courtship violence, or "date rape." After dating for two months a man and woman cuddle on her apartment couch until she senses an aggressiveness in his kiss. He slows down when she tells him to, but then starts unbuttoning her blouse. She smiles and says no—she's not in the mood, not now, and tells him so. He insists she is, and keeps fondling. She frowns, pulls away, and raises her voice. He gets angry, throws her down, and rapes her. A sad story, but true. One minute they're on the courting path, the next minute they're mortal enemies. She's a crime victim and he's a criminal.

When a man goes beyond the limits set by a woman's behavior, she should take heed. The normal courting sequence is slow, gentle, and smoothly negotiated. Even on videotape it's hard to know who is taking the lead, so synchronized are the signals. So when his grip is too strong, his kiss too lengthy, or his embrace too tight— beware. It can show he's not responding to her cues. His reaction to what she sends should be instantaneous; if not, he could be dangerous.

A woman should watch for tightened muscles in the man's arms and jaws, perspiration on his brow, mouth breathing, and all the cardiac-respiratory signs of lust. If he's not also giving her parental, caring gestures—treating her kindly with obvious softness—if he doesn't yield when she wants him to, watch out. It could be that her date has shifted into runaway sexual overdrive. Like some men at the edge of Phase Five, he could be capable of raping now and later claiming she led him into it.

If so, it's time for action. To bring him out of the sexual mode a woman should try three tactics. First, she should pull him back up to the thinking level by engaging his neocortex: "Listen, someone's at the door!" "Look, someone's peeking in the window!" "I hear Sally on the porch!" Anything to refocus his attention away from making love, back to where he'll be more likely to accept her wish to stop.

If reason fails, she should shout. As loudly as she can, close to his ear. She should give a karate master's death yell and startle him back to reality. Soft pleading won't do it. She must scream aggressively enough to make his body jerk. The sudden jerking is her cue that he's come out of the erotic spell. Again, at this point he should be more reasonable.

But if it's all turning to disaster and this once-nice man keeps coming at her red-eyed and holding her like Brutus in a Popeye cartoon, there's only one thing to do. She should persuade his brain to drop a notch below the reptilian impulses now at work—introduce him to pain. Pinch, poke, pull hair—hard—and keep yelling. Give him signals his pain centers can grasp.

In ordinary aggression, yielding—showing a submissive signal—causes the aggressor to back off, having shown his superiority. But in sexual aggression, timid signals invite rape. It's not enough to whimper or cry. Inflicting pain can be dangerous when the rapist is a total stranger. But in date rape a woman knows something about the man. And chances are he's not on the same grim trajectory as the criminal who operates in the bushes. Her date didn't plan to go this far, and it's easier to pull him out of his erotic mindset before the damage is done.

The Waning of Courtship

With Phase Five, Lovemaking, courtship officially ends. That's not to say that after the love act couples never court again. Certainly they will trade signals of tenderness and affection to preface all their future lovemaking, but they don't have to renegotiate intimacy each time from the ground up. You will see a gradual loss of wooing signals in any relationship that lasts beyond a year. Partners begin to understand each other's habits, and they don't need to signal the same information over and over again. They can relax.

We will now turn away from the phases of courtship and look more deeply at the signals of attraction. Our faces, our bodies, our clothing, the spaces we court in—all have powerful tales to tell the watchful.

Quiz

- What does Miss America have in common with Betty Boop, Tweety Bird, Minnie Mouse, and Rubber Ducky?
    a. Large eyes.
    b. A bulbous forehead.
    c. A thin neck.
- The most important feature that distinguishes Burt Reynolds, Robert Redford, and Clint Eastwood from Woody Allen is:.
    a. A small nose.   c. White teeth.
    b. Thick hair.   d. Muscles.
- Add _____ to a baby face and you create the perfect female courting machine:
    a. Prominent brow ridges.
    b. Prominent cheekbones.
    c. Prominent mid-eyelid folds.
- Because a woman's eyebrows sit higher over her eyes than a man's brows do, her face seems intrinsically "friendlier." True or false?
- If the angle between your upper lip and the bottom of your nose measures *greater* than 90 degrees, you shouldn't date anyone who measures *less* than 90. True or false?
- Which of the following women have rather large facial features that can attract men over great distances?
    a. Cheryl Tiegs.   c. Raquel Welch.
    b. Goldie Hawn.   d. Joan Crawford.

6

The Face
of Attraction

*Your face, my thane, is a book where men may
read strange matters.*

—SHAKESPEARE

Johnny Carson, Cheryl Tiegs, Richard Nixon, Aretha Franklin, Burt Reynolds, Jacqueline Onassis, Ryan O'Neal, Brooke Shields, Woody Allen, Barbara Walters, Clark Gable, Marilyn Monroe, Walter Cronkite, Sidney Poitier, Barbra Streisand, Ann-Margret—just reading the names of these media icons evokes vivid mental pictures of faces. The face, which makes up less than 5 percent of the body's total surface area, is a major carrier of personality and image. We firmly identify a person with the front of his or her head.

Generally, people respond to the face as the most important clue to an individual's character. But in courtship it counts even more. No other part of our anatomy houses as many attracting signals per square inch than the face, with its crush of features. And no other bodily surface has more sensory terminals—eyes, nose, lips, ears, and tongue—with which to decode incoming courtship signals. The face, our most "outspoken" region, is a major sender *and* receiver, a source and a target of courting messages. Boy-meets-girl comes to a head, you could say, in the face.

Like it or not, we judge people by the attractiveness of their faces. "Pretty prejudice" in courtship is worldwide. A beautiful face automatically inspires a teasing response. We react to a pleasant exterior as if it covered a pleasant interior. All through life, good-looking faces confer social advantages—cute children get better treatment in school; pretty women get warnings instead of traffic citations; handsome men go further in politics. If Hubert Humphrey had only looked more like John Kennedy he might have become president. And so it goes. Unfair, yes, but understand what people look for in a face and you can maximize your chances in courtship.

All faces have the same basic flat, round, two-eye, beak-nose, everted-lip, jutting-chin structure. To a being from Mars, human faces would look wearily alike. But to people on Earth the subtlest variation *in any measurement*— the size of a nostril, the thinness of a lip, the angle between the upper lip and the bottom of the nose, anything—is enough to make one face "beautiful" and another face "plain." Beauty is not only skin deep but also millimeters wide.

There's nothing mysterious about facial beauty. You can analyze it, list its features, sculpt it from clay, or sketch it on paper. Nor have our standards changed much since civilized man first began recording instances of facial perfection. The sculpture of Queen Nefertiti is as striking today as it was in ancient Egypt. Michelangelo's *David* has facial features women today find attractive in actors Robert Redford and Ryan O'Neal. And ugliness, too, is commonly agreed upon through history and across continents. The faces of Jimmy Durante and the Wicked

Witch of the West in *The Wizard of Oz* would be considered less than attractive in any society in any age.

Let's start with the necessary background. Before we go over the face trait by trait, we should distinguish between courtship "attractive" and beauty-contest "perfect." No one needs to look like Miss America winner Mary Ann Mobley or *Cosmopolitan's* "America's Sexiest Man," Scott Brown, to attract a mate. Ironically, picture-perfect faces often intimidate would-be partners and keep them away. The most alluring faces—those that best draw people in and keep them close—would never win a beauty contest. Ideal courting faces are those typified by the likes of TV's "Good Morning America" host, David Hartman, actress Jill Clayburgh and "Today" coanchor Jane Pauley, in all of whom cuteness, "imperfection," and "character" combine to give great courting leverage.

From Fish to Bogart and Bergman

The human face has become a courting blackboard, a wooing marquee. We shine our faces on whomever we fancy and hope that our eyes, mouth, and cheekbones will strike sparks. But the face was not always the potent, seductive organ of courtship we see today.

Our face began a slow evolution 600 million years ago from a simple opening on the leading edge of a primitive living tube. Picture the business end of a vacuum-cleaner hose and you'll understand the basic ancestral structure of the human face. Led by its yawning mouth, the free-swimming tube moved through sea water in search of food. The early "face" had no role in courtship. Its only task was to suck in nourishment. Some might think it fitting that the face originated from this primordial open mouth.

Nature gradually added nerve sensors around the mouth

for touch and seeing light. She gave her little tube a guidance system to help it find food and stay away from danger. This is why we have so many organs on our head. It is also why we lead with our faces in courtship.

Over tens of millions of years the face assumed, first in primitive fish, its now-familiar shape, two eyes and a snout set over a mouth. But the first faces were rigid. Early fish like the Devonian Ostracoderms presented rather mean-looking stone faces to the world. We owe the basic eyes-nose-mouth architecture of our face to fish, but the archaic fish face was expressionless and incapable of courtship. Its one trick was to open and close its jaws. The faces of goldfish, frogs, lizards, and birds are still frozen. These animals trade sounds, colors, odors, and body movements rather than facial expressions in order to court.

For facial expressions we owe a debt to the early mammals. About 70 million years ago nature conducted a little experiment and "freed" the faces of furry, warm-blooded animals. She "unstuck" key facial traits, and the mammalian visage came to life.

And just as soon as faces animated, after a certain primitive neck muscle, the *platysma*, grew forward over the early mammals' cheeks and spread like so many tentacles around the eyes, lips, forehead, and ears, sexual communication changed. The face became a kind of marionette that danced to the emotions. Faces moved to courtship's hormonal rhythms, and for the first time in evolutionary history animals could wink, grin, and leer.

Nowhere was the face more liberated than in the primates, the biological order we share with monkeys and apes. Primate facial muscles are incredibly complex, mobile, and expressive. Courtship messages—pro and con—emanate from simian faces as lips compress, brows lower, foreheads rise, ears flatten, tongues show, eyes widen, mouths smack, muzzles tense, lids droop, and teeth bare. In the primate face, every movement speaks.

Of course, the zenith of courting expressivity, nature's state of the art, is found in the human face. Nothing compares in subtlety or potential attractiveness. Nature designed the human countenance to be as visually seductive as any neon-bedecked Las Vegas sign. One has only to think of Rudolph Valentino's eyes, Marilyn Monroe's sugary pout, the otherworldly mouth of da Vinci's Mona Lisa, and the painful last look Bergman gives Bogart in *Casablanca*. We've come a long way from the fishes.

What Is Beauty?

As plastic surgeons know, the difference between sublime and ridiculous in a face can be measured in millimeters. The tiniest differences in scale and proportion in the facial plane can make us lust over one face and ignore another. What exactly makes a face beautiful? Why do women generally prefer Tom Selleck to Woody Allen? Why do men get more enthusiastic over Bo Derek or Catherine Deneuve than they do over Totie Fields or Phyllis Diller?

The ideal courting face in every society begins with the lean jawline of a young adult, sixteen to twenty-one years old. The facial skin is smooth, moist, unlined, and blemish free. The teeth are evenly spaced, and neither project forward nor curve inward. The jaws align without a telling overbite or underbite. The chin is neither too sloping ("chinless") nor too long ("vertical excess"), nor is it slung too far to the rear ("retrograde mandible"). The nose is not so large that it competes for attention with the other features. Around the world, attractive faces are symmetrical and balanced.

In addition to these pancultural criteria, ideal courting faces also display "mosaic" architecture. That is, they are composite blends of three design features: (1) "infantile cute" (like the face of gymnast Cathy Rigby), (2) "mature adult'' (like actress Joan Crawford), and (3) ''rugged and strong'' (like actor Jack Palance). The average face is an amalgam of the three features.

In courtship, all things being equal, certain mixtures work better than others. Model Cheryl Tiegs's mosaic, for example, with its large forehead, wide-set eyes, tiny nose, vertically ''deficient'' (*i.e.,* baby-size) chin, and high-flying cheekbones, is attractive because it combines maturity and cuteness in the right mix. Actor Burt Reynolds's face, on the other hand, is a blend of infant, adult, and rugged features—it's a boy's face with conspicuous, adult cheekbones and a Joe Palooka jaw. Without the sharp angles and wideness of these bony structures, his face would seem even more boyish, like Johnny Carson's.

The ultimate ''fierce'' face has rugged, overscale, bony brows and a loaf-size jaw, like that of World Boxing Association heavyweight champion, Larry Holmes. In Holmes's football-player-fierce face, strength overshadows the other design features. But when facial strength shows without wholly overpowering the infantile or the mature features, we say it has ''rugged good looks.'' Such a mosaic is worn by Jack Palance, whose face is handsome but so bare-knuckles rugged it should be kept in a holster.

Attractive women's faces combine cuteness (infantile traits) with prominent cheekbones (a sign of maturity) without showing much in the way of strength. Bo Derek has the classic blend. But when all three design features show in a female face the result can be striking. Both Sophia Loren and Raquel Welch have big-bore, ''long-distance'' courting faces that can drop a man where he stands from across a room.

Baby Face. All pretty women and all handsome men have several key babylike traits embroidered in their faces. The infantile (or ''neotenous'') features are courtship's most-active ingredients. The cuteness is what attracts.

The amount of "infant appeal" in a face determines how much magic it works in courtship. Nature programmed us to respond with love and cuddles to baby traits. Seeing an infant's soft, round, hairless face, bulbous forehead, large wide-set eyes, button nose, chubby cheeks, small mouth, and wee chin (as well as its thin neck, narrow shoulders, and high-pitch voice) makes us feel like nuzzling and cooing. One look at the cute little face and our hearts go out to it.

Nature designed adults so that the very sight of an infant's buttery face automatically releases warm, caring feelings. It's to a baby's advantage to attach himself to us emotionally with cuteness. Otherwise we might abandon the wee one the first time it cried or messed a diaper. A baby with a face like Leonid Brezhnev's might receive less than total, loving care.

Infantlike features can "cuten" almost any face. You can even tease cuddle reactions from people with rubber, plastic, and wooden objects decorated with immaturity signals. As toy manufacturers know, the baby-face template has a magic drawing power. Mickey Mouse, Minnie Mouse, Kewpie doll, Barbie and Ken dolls, teddy bears, Tweety Bird, rubber duckies, and E.T. all have neotenous, baby-cute faces that draw loving responses from both children and adults.

Look closely at the faces of Diana Ross, Marilyn Monroe, Goldie Hawn, Miss USA, Miss Spain, Miss Thailand, Miss Universe, Miss Here, or Miss There and you'll see the infantile template broadcast its message: "Cuddle me." Lamp-size eyes spaced far apart; petal-soft, wrinkle-free skin; bud nose; large-vertical (that is, nonsloping) forehead; small jaws—feminine beauty reduces to the visual dimensions of Betty Boop.

Grown-Up Face. Betty Boop is a bit *too* infantile, though, with her saucer eyes, puffed-out cheeks, and bing-cherry mouth stuck on her chin. She's a cartoon caricature of courtship's neoteny principle. If men actually *were* attracted to raw immaturity, a greater number of little girls would be in danger of sexual advances than there already are.

As a sexual draw, neoteny is an area in which nature has not worked out all the bugs. A man's taste for baby traits sometimes grades pervertedly into "pedophilia," sexual desire for children. Like the inevitable back pain that is a by-product of our too-sudden upright posture, we suffer the insults of child molesters because nature made visual immaturity too attractive, too quickly, in our evolution.

Most men find mature women more attractive than young girls. None but the sorriest pedophiliac could fall in love with a woman who had an oversize version of the Gerber Baby's head on her shoulders. And few women would want a full complement of toddler traits showing in their faces, like Lucy in the *Peanuts* comic strip. So nature did some blending. Starting with the infantile template, nature added mature signals to keep "woman" distinct from "girl." She did this while at the same time retaining immaturity's innate drawing power, and designed a composite, an "adult baby face."

Basically the idea is this: start with the budding features of the baby template. Add on mature traits, without changing the heart-melting eyes-nose-mouth pattern in the infant scheme, and you've got it: generic beauty.

Nature shapes the female face in a fascinating way. As a girl changes into a woman, her skin's fat content thins so that her facial bones begin to show. Her nose cartilage hardens, sometimes sharpens, but the nose stays proportionally small. After puberty a woman's cheekbones flare, her lower jaw widens and squares under the ears, and her chin develops a bony prominence, an osseous knob.

Generic beauty. Attractive women everywhere have the same bone structure. Ideal courting faces seem to be stretched tightly over outstretching, "sprung" cheekbones. This, and the lower jaw, which widens and squares at the sides, along with the mature forehead, which slants backward now over the eyebrows (it's not quite the vertical cliff it was earlier), constitute the adult "frame" for the babylike eyes, babylike mouth, and smooth skin.

And what of the nose? It stays small. Should the female nose enlarge, as the male's does, it would only interfere with the beguiling eyes-cheeks-mouth triumverate. Interfere, yes, but perhaps not damage. Remember, we are looking at the face as a *courting* medium, not as raw material for beauty contests. The standards differ. Impose a queen-size nose on an already attractive feminine face and a man still admires the gestalt, just as many men praise the uncommon beauty of Barbra Streisand and Princess Diana.

Fierce Face. But what about masculine beauty? Surprisingly, it's the same. Everything said so far about the female face also holds true for men. Immaturity and adultness are valid principles in the male face, too. Women respond to disarming, wide-open boyish faces, such as those of Johnny Carson, Bob Newhart, Jack Nicklaus, and Phil Donahue, because they all have the right combination of grown-up and childlike traits. Men lower on the adult scale, men whose bulbous foreheads and other undiluted infantile features give them almost a baby-face look—Paul Williams, Mickey Rooney, Dick Cavett, Wally Cox, and Don Knotts, for instance—are less "handsome." But such men can appeal more directly to a woman's maternal instincts, so the male baby face is not as unappealing as some might think.

The most effective male courting faces, the truly handsome, are those that combine immaturity and adultness with "ferocity," the third design feature. Faces from the Tom Selleck, Clint Eastwood, Clark Gable, and Burt

Reynolds mold combine all three designs in their rugged good looks.

Analyze Burt Reynolds's face and you find the wide-set eyes, relatively small nose, and full lips of the infantile template. To this add an angular jawbone, a prominent chin, and projecting cheekbones, all adult features, and you have a basic "good-looking" face, one Raquel Welch or any woman would be proud to wear in a feminine version.

Now, to make the face rugged, sculpt into the skull certain "fierce" traits, without disturbing the good looks already there. First, enlarge the whole face, make it wider and longer to amplify the overall effect. Size turns up the facial volume, as it were. Second, work in lumpy ridges over the eyes, so the eyebrows rest on visible, bony shelves; and with your thumbs push his eyes inward to give them a deep-set appearance. Third, holding firmly onto his jawbone with both hands, pull down to make his face below the nose significantly larger than it is in women. Finally, scratch in four or five authority-connoting horizontal wrinkles on the forehead, stipple in moustache and beard hair, thicken the eyebrows, and you've created a superlative courting face, one admired by millions in magazines and movies, and on TV—a media icon.

Rugged good looks say, in effect, "I'm cute and lovable, sexually mature, and tough, all in one irresistible package." O. J. Simpson, James Coburn, Lee Marvin, Ronald Reagan, and Muhammad Ali have such magnum courting faces.

Woody Allen, Richard Nixon, and Spiro Agnew do not. There's not one "fierce" trait, for example, in Woody Allen's small, narrow face. The overscale nose dominates its few infantile features, though the out-rolling lower lip, nearly twice as large as the upper, gives him a pouted look women like. His eyes, chin, and sloping forehead are comparatively small, in contrast to Reynolds's, and Woody Allen has no visible cheekbones. Indeed, few courting messages are broadcast from his face, and the mosaic makes him perfect for the comical "unloved" role he plays so brilliantly.

Richard Nixon has a face at cross-purposes with itself. Basically adult, there's not a single cuddly trait visible anywhere on its slumping, jowly surface. His eyes are small, and the background noise of wrinkles and pouches drowns out his mouth. The aerodynamic nose strongly draws on onlooker's eye, of course, but it's the caricatured bottom half of his face, the "apples" in his cheeks that take attention away from the cheekbones, an effect that pushes Nixon's face beyond the pale of effectiveness in courtship. If he'd had a Clint Eastwood face fewer people might have kicked him around.

And former Vice-President Spiro Agnew's face . . . well, the best way to describe it is with a train metaphor. Map Agnew's features on the front end of a modern turbine locomotive and you capture the inherent force of a face that comes at you even as it stands still. With no infant traits, few adult features—mainly potato nose and watermelon jaw—Agnew's potent face seems to leap at you like a boxing glove.

Facial Caps, Stems, and Pieces

Granted, boy-meets-girl is easier for those whose design features harmonize. In courtship, the basic Burt Reynolds or Raquel Welch physiognomy gives a person more sexual choices than a Woody Allen or a Phyllis Diller face may give. But every face has its better traits. As John Merrick, the Elephant Man, taught us, no one need be unloved because of a flawed exterior. Anyone can play up the features that work and play down the less-inspiring ones. Nobody mentioned so far (except, alas, Merrick) has gone without a sex life.

Let's look at the face trait by trait.

Hair. When you first walk into a singles' bar you see wall-to-wall hair. Hair is to human courting what tail feathers are to the peacock's: a medium of sexual expression. Not only does a woman's soft, fluffy hair draw a basic tactile response from men, not only do her shiny, bouncing tendrils attract men's eyes, but the fact that she makes the effort to groom her hair is a message in itself. Styled hair shows she wants to be noticed, and men unconsciously appreciate the news.

Hair is so expressive that few women limit its possibilities by cutting it short or pulling it into a tight bun. Those who play down their tresses give an implicit message that they are not seriously courting. The short ducktails some lesbians wear, for instance, not only show manliness but also show men they're not interested in a heterosexual liaison.

Women wear their locks longer than men so their hairstyles will contrast with men's. Contrast—signaling what you're *not*—is part of the meaning transmitted by hair. In the 1960s, hippy men grew long hair so they would contrast with the Ivy League "straights," and then grew beards to contrast with the long-haired hippy womenfolk. In the 1980s, "new-wave" men cut their hair short to contrast with the hippies, trim their sideburns off to contrast with 1950s Elvis Presley hound-dog greasers, and dye their locks blue, pink, or purple to further establish their contrasted identities. There's little a man won't do for courtship's sake.

Hair gives the face a perceptual border. If there's a picture hanging somewhere nearby, mentally remove the top part of the frame. If it then seems unbalanced, it is, because the brain will perceive the picture's contents as being somehow less "together" than when they were all tied up inside the frame. This is why men fear balding—not only because hair loss is a sign of age but because it makes their facial features seem "unframed." Without a thatchy border on top, a man's eyes will seem smaller in proportion to his yawning forehead. Unframed, the whole, fleshy landscape seems larger, and the eyes shrink in proportion to the gestalt. But it's not all bad. Baldness gives the head an infantile appeal which makes a hairless man easier to approach. That, and the tactile urgency the exposed, shiny skin evokes in women—they want to pat or kiss the bald pate—can make baldness something of an asset. Contrary to popular opinion, male hair loss is not necessarily a handicap.

But for women a full head of hair is essential. And not only for the gender contrast. Skillfully cut bangs cover and "shrink" the female forehead and proportionally reduce the size of the face. The effect scales down the nose and makes the eyes more prominent. This and the soft curtain of overhanging hair set up a tactile resonance with the smooth skin. The only women who can wear their hair pulled back, entirely off the top and sides of the face, are those with flawless, vertical, unlined Mona Lisa foreheads. If your facial features and forehead wouldn't stand alone, that is, look good under conditions of total baldness, wear your hair at least to collar level, fluffed out at the sides, with your bangs no higher than an inch above your eyebrows. That's the optimal courting frame because it showcases the strongest traits: the eyes, lips, and cheekbones.

According to folk wisdom, gentlemen prefer blondes while women prefer men who are dark. We can speculate that blondeness suggests youthful innocence, because Euro-American babies so often have light-colord hair. Blond women, therefore, may seem more childlike than brunettes. Men with blond hair often consider their image unattractive, as actor Michael Caine once admitted, perhaps because of the connotations of immaturity. Dark hair, which is less babylike, gives the face a more visible, contrasting frame and with the accompanying conspicuous eyebrows, makes a person seem more authoritative. But this is still speculative because the critical differences between Tab Hunter and Rock Hudson hair have not been seriously studied. Consider, though, that if *Dracula* star Frank Langella had been blond and blue-eyed, the whole cast of his personality would somehow reverse. Which is to say, Robert Redford could never play a satanic role.

Hair transmits too many courting messages and affects the facial gestalt too dramatically to be left to fad, fashion, or chance. A skilled hairdresser is a must; a professional stylist can analyze your face objectively—you, yourself, cannot—and help you build the right frame for your features. To cap the face artfully it's worth paying top dollar.

Wrinkles. Why do women calk and grout facial wrinkles with creams in courtship, but men leave theirs alone? Why are crow's-feet, lines, and creases somehow "wrong" on female faces but OK on males?

Nothing about wrinkles is inherently ugly. No one, for instance, gets upset by cheek dimples or by the philtrum (the upper lip's beveled groove) or by the mid-eyelid fold (the wrinkle that runs right above the top of the eyelash when the lid is open). Even babies have dimples, lip grooves, and lid lines. . . .

Babies have them, yes—and that's why nobody paints over these particular wrinkles. But every other line the face picks up with age threatens the template. Forehead lines, nasolabio lines (which run from the nostril bulbs to the mouth corners), and the baggy crepe lines under the lower lids compete for viewer attention, and few things in nature can draw an eye as powerfully as lines. What's wrong with wrinkles, in short, is that they are just so much linear "noise" in the system.

Women moisturize, powder, and cream their lines to

keep the infantile features showing through. Cosmetics help damp down the static, as it were. And nowadays makeup application has become such a science—or at the least such a sophisticated art form—that any courting woman who omits cosmetics for political reasons is only cheating herself. Competing with skillfully made-up women, even natural beauties seem plain.

What keeps some women from exploring makeup is seeing so many others on whom the blush, lipstick, eyeliner, and overdone mascara look conspicuous, garish, or sloppy. But such observations miss the point. Cosmetics are less useful as facial decorations—like flocked snow on a Christmas tree—than they are as aids to bring out a face's natural beauty. Put another way, when eyelash liner goes on too thickly it calls attention to *itself* rather than to the lash it accents. But when powders, creams, and so on draw attention to velvety, seamless skin without seeming to be there, they confer a powerful courting advantage.

Most men don't edit out their own facial lines because the infantile template is not as crucial to their success in courtship. The smooth, soft baby-face look isn't necessary. Indeed, some wrinkles even make the male face *more* attractive. What woman would erase all the lines from Robert Redford's face? Certain wrinkles add fierceness to the male mask. According to popular belief, lines give a man's face "character."

The vertical-scowl creases between the eyebrows, along with the nasolabio furrows, put a "mean" look on a man's face. The horizontal forehead wrinkles that show when he raises his eyebrows add authority to his stare. A stern, corrugated brow makes a man's words weightier, as TV evangelists Oral Roberts and Billy Graham know.

Because wrinkles that highlight facial expressions or add power to a face work for men there's no reason to hide them. But *non*functional wrinkles—under-eye bags, cheek jowls, crepelike lip lines, and "turkey gobbler" folds on the neck (which create a less-defined angle between the neck and the chin)—do as little for men as they do for women in the sexual domain: nothing, in a word. They only compete with the courting signals themselves.

The Nose. Our freestanding nose—a rather oddlooking, fleshy organ from any angle—is beautiful in no one's book. Whoever comments about a member of the opposite sex, "Nice nose"? Nobody, ever, because the nose is mainly esteemed for what it is *not*. Which is to say, a person's nose goes unnoticed unless it is a bit *too* something—too droopy, too large, too red, too bulbous, that is, too high-profile.

Leaf through any women's magazine and the status of the feminine nose is quickly revealed. Incredibly tiny, inconspicuous noses wink up from the models' faces in the ads. When you see a model's nose head-on, only the nostrils tell you it's actually there. Cosmetics ads take it a step further and reduce the mannequins' already small noses to the vanishing point. Which is the whole idea. Makeup subjugates the female nose, tames the wedge so the eminence seems to melt into the flat. The lips and eyes are left to dominate the milk-and-blush surface like fresh-decals.

The message is clear in these pages: Nose, get thee behind me. Even in men's magazines the nose gets bad press. Cigarette ads feature rugged, square-faced men with skin like unpolished marble and surprisingly dainty noses. Liquor ads show men with deeply clefted chins, overscale jaws, thin mouths, brow ridges you could cut a finger on, and . . . diminutive noses. With saber-narrow bridges and knot-hard tips, the noses on those roughhewn faces are *tiny*.

The sight of so many little noses in the printed media, in movies, and on TV has made most of us vaguely upset with our own nose. The proboscis has become the most self-criticized part of the face. Men play down too-prominent noses with moustaches, beards, bouffant hairstyles, and longer bangs. Women hide their noses by wearing fluffy hair, or they take advantage of certain cosmetic techniques to "down-sculpt" the nose. Those with noses that make it too embarrassing to sit for caricature sketches at the county fair often resort to plastic surgery, which is now safe, routine, effective, and comparatively inexpensive.

But no one with a merely "presidential" or "queen-size" proboscis need despair. A large nose never stopped anyone in courtship, no matter what the media may suggest. Size competes with the baby-face template, to be sure, but adds character and interest at the same time. A face with a larger nose is often more intriguing than one with only a baby-size nib. The noses of Barbra Streisand and Cher give their faces a unique beauty, and also allow them to wear more striking, dramatic eye makeup which would overpower small-nosed faces. On a man, a large nose, like that of Teddy Roosevelt, Lyndon Johnson, Charles de Gaulle, or John Kenneth Galbraith, can add an appealing connotation of authority.

Eyebrows. Facial distinctiveness and character count as much in courtship as good looks. The cloned sameness of fashion-model and beauty-queen faces undeniably works in the wooing game, quite nicely in fact, but uniqueness can work better. Originality keeps a face from seeming "blah." Picture-perfect Ken and Barbie doll faces quickly seem boring after the shock of all that seamless beauty wears off.

Even in professional modeling it's the unusual face that catapults a rank-and-file model to fame. Take eyebrows. We've seen how male brows sit low on the orbit, making a man's eyes seem more deeply set and giving him a piercing gaze, a more threatening stare. And we've seen how a woman's lighter, thinner brow flares upward as it arcs off the side of her face, giving her a chronically raised brow that mimics the universally friendly "eyebrow flash" of recognition. Beautiful women have built-in "come-hither," lifted brows. And fashion models have the highest of all.

At least they did until a young model named Brooke Shields came along with dark, low brows and rewrote the rules. Her deep-set eyes pool out from under singularly lush eyebrows set in a face perched ambivalently on the cusp between girl and woman, a face makeup nudges into the grown-up courting world. With its uniqueness, Brooke Shields's face broke the mold. Now, high-vaulting eyebrows like Doris Day's are not absolutely required. Women need not pluck and pencil to achieve crescent-shaped surprise lines that seem to lift into the hairline, or stencil on the drop-forged killer brows of Joan Crawford. Rim-hugging brows are OK—better, in fact, because they are symbolic: they look like Brooke's.

Eyes, Cheekbones, and Chins. Large, widely spaced eyes, projecting cheekbones, and a prominent chin can make any face more attractive. Place a small nose in the picture and you get a Cheryl Tiegs, Mia Farrow, Jon Voight, or Robert Redford face. Plastic surgeons often tighten the baggy skin under a person's eyes, insert silicone cheekbone implants, and "augment" the chin at the same time, because facial beauty rests squarely on these three features.

But the face compensates for its shortcomings. Most men cannot resist the "all-American" face, that is, the wholesome one with Jane Pauley eyes and an OK chin but inconspicuous cheekbones. Such a face would never win a beauty contest, but it's highly attractive from a courting point of view. The peaches-and-cream, milkmaid face of English-born actress Julie Andrews is of this genre. The beguiling eyes, narrow cheekbones, and too-prominent chin give her long face an appealing, but nonseductive, cast—

one reason her sex-kitten roles have never seemed convincing.

Still, cheekbones get top billing in American courtship. When they don't actually fly from the high trapeze, women optically lift, spread, and swell them with blush. The reason prominent cheekbones figure so powerfully in male and female beauty, in all cultures, is that they are one of the few traits that make a face sexually mature, on the one hand, without disturbing the infantile template on the other.

Swelling the cheekbones is one thing. Swelling the cheeks themselves is a different matter. Too much fat in the face balloons the cheeks, jowls the jawline, and makes the chin seem to founder in a sea of loose flesh. There's nothing inherently ugly about facial fat itself, but when too much adipose tissue threatens the eyes-cheekbones-chin trio it's time to think about dieting. These alluring facial traits project too much of your courting image for you to mask them.

In this connection it is instructive, looking around a singles' bar, to see that only a few men and fewer women have on glasses. People realize that glasses interfere with the natural appeal of the eyes, the most potent of all courting signs. But glasses—especially those that don't compliment the face—damage more than eye appeal. Glasses spanning the temples and orbital rims add lines in all the wrong places, over the cheekbones and across the eyebrows. Not only do they interfere with these critical traits, but glasses also emphasize the nose—make it look bigger, like squeezed putty—and deemphasize the chin. It would be hard to design anything more damaging to one's visual image. Potentially damaging, that is, because a competent oculist can help you choose glasses that will enhance your facial features. Money spent on hairstyling and on the right frames—rounded for women, squared with a double bar (to mark the brow ridge) for men—is the best investment anyone can make in courtship.

Lips. Careful film studies of eye movements reveal that when we look at a person's face, our eyes busily track up, down, back, and forth over the whole facial surface. Nothing is unseen. Eyes bounce from feature to feature, from cheekbone to hairline to eyebrow, back to the hairline, and so on, never resting long in one spot. A man spends an average of five seconds to take in the features of an unfamiliar woman's face.

The three most-examined traits, the landmarks our eyes revisit over and over, are the eyes and the mouth. Our line of sight caroms among the eyes and mouth in a triangular path, like a pinball. Eyes, we saw earlier, have an innate appeal; babies only weeks old show a special sensitivity to eyespots painted on white cardboard.

But what draws our gaze to a person's mouth? The answer is . . . the lips. Lips capture our attention because their outrolled surface functions as a natural courting signal. Lips evolved so that infant mammals could suckle. Babies' mouths need a muscular, airtight seal to draw mother's milk from the nipple. But the human *everted* lip is unique among the primates. With their high visibility our lips are something rather special.

Sexual excitement may cause the lips to blush. Therefore coloring the lips in red shades draws male eyes to the mouth and suggests receptivity. It's not by accident that most lip cosmetics are crimson.

Full, generous lips also further the baby look. Indeed, to men, certain female lips, such as those of French actress Brigitte Bardot, that retain the infantile "beak," can be extra alluring. The mid portion of a baby's lips is better developed than the outer portions, to facilitate sucking, and the muscles make the middle part puff out like a beak.

When it's present, the "baby beak" helps give feminine lips a seductive, irresistible, pouted look.

Women often exaggerate the upper lip's connection with the grooved philtrum by "notching" it with lipstick to play up the pouted look. Outlining the whole mouth perimeter with lip liner helps create a sharp line of contrast that also draws a man's eyes. Some people complain because their upper lip is thinner than the lower lip, as is the case with CBS news anchor Dan Rather. But far from being a handicap, a puffed-out lower lip also creates the "pout" both men and women find attractive.

Ears. The less said about ears, with their nightmarish, twisting folds and tortured creases, the better. If an ear is small and hugs the side of the head, fine. But when it asserts itself like a teacup handle, or insists on jiggling its oversized lobe, let the hair drop over it like a merciful curtain.

When exposed, small soft ears suggest vulnerability and don't take attention away from the more-attractive parts of the face. Around the world both men and women decorate their ears to improve their courting image. Earrings are the most common adornments, but earrings actually work less as ornaments than as visual "bumper cushions." Ear jewelry pulls an onlooker's eye back and forth across the wearer's face.

All you can do with your own ears is reveal, decorate, or hide them. But don't overlook the message your partner's ears tell. Of all the body's parts, ear flaps are the first to blush. So sensitive are these thin-skinned organs to embarrassment, modesty, and shame that they bear close watching in courtship. Seeing a man's or a woman's ears redden is more reliable than any lie detector in showing you've touched a nerve. Face to face, therefore, suddenly red ears on someone you've just met are a positive sign. You've triggered a submissive reaction in courting centers deep within your partner's brain.

Best Face Forward

The face is only one aspect of a person's total "presentation of self." A key part, but hardly the most important thing in courtship. The body, clothing, postures, and poise together count for more than the front of the head.

Nevertheless, it's good strategy to put forward the best possible face. This doesn't mean trying to look like Catherine Deneuve or Frank Langella, or like any other media icon. Few women have the wax-museum-perfect face of TV's Lynda (Wonder Woman) Carter. Few male faces come together quite like Tom Selleck's.

That hardly matters, though, because courtship is like tennis or football—one part natural ability and nine parts effort. Do as any serious player does and analyze your game, its strengths and weaknesses. Study your face's design features, play up the better traits, and play down the liabilities.

Spend time thinking about the best way to frame your face. Get outside opinions—you're too habituated to your own face to be objective. Remember that good looks *and* personality are attractive. Keep your face healthy and well groomed, because both these qualities have deep roots in primate courtship.

The most attractive face has an expression on it. Forget the suave, serious, "cool" look. Aloof, sober expressions don't work well in courtship. Nature didn't spend millions of years giving us expressive faces so that we would stand around looking like sophisticated reptiles. But not just any expression will do. Don't tighten your mouth, or unconsciously "chew," or move your lips around as though you're chronically ready to sneeze. Practice your best Jack Nicholson killer smile or your best Lily Tomlin manic grin. Better than cuteness, the smiling face draws people from every part of the strutting ground.

Quiz

- Below the neck a woman's most alluring trait is:
  - a. Her bosom.
  - b. Her derriere.
  - c. Her hourglass figure.
- Women want their men to have:
  - a. Washboard abdominals.
  - b. An Arnold Schwarzenegger build.
  - c. Strong, sensitive hands.
- Female breasts stay swollen after puberty because they're not just milk-producing organs but also sexual signals. True or false?
- According to the feminine world view, a man's buns are less erotic, or sexy, than "friendly" and "vulnerable." True or false?
- Among the many feminine orb signals are:
  - a. The tops of the upper arms.
  - b. The calves.
  - c. The elbows.
- Men have nearly twice as many sexual scent glands as women have. True or false?

Below the Neck—
How Bodies Attract

Mama Mia!

Go to secluded Black's Beach in San Diego, a stretch of Pacific Ocean devoted to nude sunbathing, unfurl a towel on the hot, white sand, and with your best sense of Olympian detachment observe the naked bodies on parade. Men walk the shore timidly, their swagger gone, their heads tipped forward, and their shoulders slumped. Women seem less inhibited but still reserved as they bounce and frolic in the surf. The human body, with its upright, bipedal posture, unfurred skin, and exposed genital organs, especially in the male, looks soft and vulnerable on the seashore, a bit pathetic, like an oyster out of its shell.

When Mother Nature stood us upright on two legs millions of years ago and radically thinned our hairy coats to the present functional nudity, human sexual signals changed. In most four-legged animals, the chest (or brisket), underbelly, and genitalia are covered with fur and concealed beneath the body. Dogs and cats seem almost sexless until they roll over. But with our own vertical posture and hairless skin these once-covered body parts now show. And when we come together face to face on Black's Beach, there's no getting away from chests, soft bellies, and genital complications. Of course, we keep our eyes politely raised, but the conspicuous sexual signals invade our vision strongly enough to keep us unsettled, guarded. On this beach it's all too obvious: a human being doesn't have to roll belly up for one to read the sex.

Serious, card-carrying nudists will tell you that nakedness is natural. It's clothes, they say, that are abnormal. But around the world just the opposite is true. Men and women in nearly every society wear clothing, if only a pubic apron or a genital covering of some kind—a penis sheath, a breach cloth, or a simple skirt—to cover the sexual organs. Exposed genitals are too upsetting in the stream of behavior and only get in the way. Clothing may have originated more than anything else as a kind of sexual mask.

Imagine Dan Rather, nude, quoting the Dow Jones average from a chair in front of his news desk. The sexual messages his body would send out over the airwaves would compete strongly with our full appreciation of the evening report. And if we believe Kinsey, who found that most women dislike seeing male genitalia, the female audience would find frontal nudity repellent on the screen. Husbands, too, would resent another man's bald sexual message invading their living room, setting their wives' teeth on edge. Or imagine a voluptuous PTA president sitting on a stool, nude, her gavel in hand, raising serious issues at the monthly meeting. Men might find her words less stimulating than her movements.

Clothing works as hairy coats and four-legged postures once did to regulate the flow of sexual information. Today's artificial coverings do an exceptional job of subduing the more blatant transmissions. In a crowded bus you might not even think about the many genitalia within reach. That man standing close to your seat holding the handrail, his crotch inches from your face—well, we all owe a debt to the inventor of pants.

Without dense, hairy coats, human bodies have become more expressive, both visually and tactilely, than they ever were when they were covered with fur. Stand a naked man next to a peacock, and at first glance there's no comparison. The human anatomy looks decidedly dull. But examine the unadorned body a bit more closely and you'll find a hundred sexual signals in the fleshy terrain, many more than you'd find in the exotic-hued bird.

Tactile cues are among the human body's most powerful messages. In lovemaking, hairless skin presses together until the brain feels as if it, itself, is being caressed with velvet gloves. Furry animals mate without much preliminary touching. It's a little like zipping up in a down-filled sleeping bag and negotiating sexual congress through a vent hole. Touching is such a potent part of our sexuality, and excessive body hair such a liability, that men and women shave, depilate, or even destroy the hair root for the sake of smoothness.

Without fur, our body's secondary sexual traits, the differences that begin to show after puberty—male and female hips, breasts, muscles, necks, and so on—have become more present to view. A dense coat of hair, such as chimps and gorillas have, would only cover up thin waists and large biceps. Left uncovered, however, these gender signals broadcast clearly; even tiny contrasts between men and women show, and it's precisely these bodily differences that we consider attractive. By standing us up and baring our chests, tummies, bottoms, and legs, nature made our bodies more exciting to behold and touch. From the neck down, from the Adam's apple to the toes, the human body broadcasts sexual messages with an urgency we're just beginning to understand.

The Body Beautiful

The first thing people ask when a baby is born is, "Girl or Boy?" Gender is humankind's oldest, deepest, and most vital social category. We pigeonhole everyone we meet into the appropriate sexual slot without even thinking.

To determine the sex of a newborn, we look at his or her *primary* sexual traits. Penis indicates "boy," and vaginal labia, "girl." Sometimes in a baby girl you see a slight swelling of the breast tissues. But apart from these cues newborns look alike, because both boys and girls start out in the embryonic stage with bodies that are basically female. Apart from the genitals themselves, male and female babies basically give off the same feminine signals.

In childhood, visible sex differences bloom as the male hormone androgen works its influence and literally makes a boy out of a girl. Estrogen, the feminizing hormone, acts on the female template and pulls the body further along a path to womanhood. Yet, apart from the genital organs and the cultural cues present in clothing and length of hair, it may be hard to tell if the ten-year-old standing in front of you is a boy or a girl. From courtship's point of view, immaturity is a condition of natural unisex.

As puberty approaches, gender contrasts erupt in a frenzy, and hormones radically masculinize or feminize the adolescent body. *Secondary* sexual signals sprout on trunks and limbs that were childlike months before. Male and female anatomies come on-line reproductively between the ages of eleven and fifteen, and external signals telegraph the news with a vengeance.

After puberty, young men and women grow further and further apart. Men don't become twice as large as women— as happens in the mountain gorilla, where a 450-pound male can weigh twice what a female weighs—but the differences are still marked. Women's bodies become adapted to child-bearing. Breasts grow, hips widen, and fatty tissue builds on bottoms and thighs as a food reserve for the fetus. The layer of fat beneath a woman's skin softens the visibility of muscle and bone and gives her body a complement of seductively rounded "orb" signals.

Like the female face, the female body has built into it several "infant appeals"—babylike features that attract men by suggesting immaturity. The baby template, the *kinderschema,* as it is known, shows in a woman's smaller stature, thinner neck, narrower shoulders, smoother and more nearly hairless skin, and in her limbs, which are smaller in proportion to her torso. The shorter legs, some have proposed, along with the slightly "bowlegged" carrying angle the femur assumes with the pelvic girdle, can make a woman's gait "clumsier" than a man's, so even her walk is a kind of immaturity signal.

Men's bodies are specialized for running, throwing, hunting, and fighting. Just as the male face grows larger and heavier—"fierce"—for bluffing other men in courtship, a man's body also enlarges to intimidate rivals. Like bigger noses, larger jaws, hardening facial lines, and beards, a man's muscles and thicker skeletal frame suggest masculine "strength in reserve."

Men are heavier and stronger, have bigger hearts and lungs, more blood hemoglobin, more muscle tissue, and less body fat than women have. A man has longer legs, bigger feet, longer forearms, and thicker hands than a woman, all of which once made him a more efficient hunter and still make him a fighter—of *other men.* Macho, we'll see, is very much a man-to-man thing.

In courtship these gender contrasts help to make the male and female bodies attractive. Beauty standards, for the most part, are uniform worldwide. As we have seen, in any society the body beautiful starts with the frame of a healthy, clear-skinned seventeen-to-twenty-two-year-old in whom the full array of secondary sexual traits shows. Young adult bodies attract because they are the most fertile. The only substantial beauty feature cultures differ on is thin versus heavy. But even the fat-skinny dimension has narrow limits. When emaciation or obesity interferes with the secondary sexual traits—when belly eclipses hip or when slimness causes the breasts to shrink—courtship appeal wanes.

Sexual World View

Before we look at the body to see which parts attract and which do not, a word about sexual "world view." Men and women see as if through different lenses. It would be worthwhile to put on the other sex's courting glasses and look at the world their way. But swapping world views is hardly an easy matter. The best we can do is to compare notes.

Let's set a scene at a fancy resort. You're outside on the pool deck on a hot summer day, sitting at a small table under an umbrella. You have a note pad in front of you and a pencil in your hand, and everyone is a stranger. Now, as you sip a cool drink, make a detailed list of what you like and dislike in swimsuited members of the opposite sex. Take ten minutes. Then exchange lists and you'll get an idea of how men and women decipher each other below the neck.

On every man's pad you'll find "figure"—chest, waist, hips, and legs—not merely listed, but sometimes ranked more important than the face. A man looks at a face for one or two seconds, then his eyes quickly drop below the neck to assess the quality of a woman's hemispherical "orb" signals. This done, his eyes go back up to the face, then drop down again to the "orbs" (the shoulders, breasts, and derriere). Finally he concludes his hasty inventory and evaluates the fine points: the smoothness of the skin, the turn of an ankle, the shape of a hand, the luster of the hair.

A man's list will be straightforward. You'll see an objective inventory of those feminine parts with which he would like to become better acquainted in bed. Men respond immediately to the visual cues. A man's courting world view is truly a *view*, an eyeful, an almost-overzealous concern with the female body as a landscape to be explored visually. A man mentally undresses a well-composed woman seconds after seeing her for the first time, whether she responds to him or not. The "orbs" and the curvilinear dimensions of the female body—the secondary-sexual gerrymandering itself—tantalizes and attracts him.

On a woman's note pad you'll find "eyes"—"friendly eyes" (crinkles in the corners and a prominent, "raised" lower eyelid fold), "sexy eyes" (deep-set with long, dark lashes), "absorbing eyes" ("he looks at me and draws me in")—coming before muscles or body shape. Responsive eyes attract women, which brings us to the first difference in courting world view. The feminine notion of what beckons and beguiles has a *personal* quality to it. Responsiveness and sensitivity count. "Do his eyes say he likes me?" is a key question to a woman. If the answer is yes, she's more likely to judge the rest of his body. If it's no, however, even the most-appealing physique seems less desirable.

Next on her list come "hands," "tall," "nice shoulders," "energy," and "buns," but not necessarily in that order. Notice that "big muscles," "macho," "tough," and "cool" don't show up anywhere on the pad. Although some men work hard to pump up and define their muscles, most women don't care. In fact, a flat, smooth stomach looks better through the female lens than lumpy, washboardlike abdominals. According to the feminine world view a man's muscles are not the irresistible signals he assumes they are.

The biggest difference in world view, then, is between "objective" and "subjective." Men inventory a woman's tangible body cues, tally them item by item, and judge her physical charm on a scale of one to ten. And they mistakenly assume that women use the same criteria to score men. But women neither reflexively disrobe nor mentally jump into bed with unfamiliar men. Rather, they read the subjective signals of masculine character, the sensitivity and tempered strength revealed in a man's hands, wide shoulders, and kind eyes. A woman considers the male "core" that draws her in. Her subjectively interpreted signals have little to do with lovemaking per se; they help to make a relationship personal first and sexual second. Men, on the other hand, reverse the process and see women's features in a harsh, erotic light. They think about temperament only *after* they've sized up the potential for lovemaking.

Body Signals

The Neck. One of the first things you notice when you hold a Barbie doll in one hand and a Ken doll in the other is that Barbie's neck is thinner. By exaggerating the natural differences in neck size, Mattel, Inc., makes Barbie seem prettier and more feminine than Ken.

In proportion to the head, a woman's neck is longer and slimmer than a man's. Although we may not consciously see the size difference, the neck has become a pivotal sign of feminine beauty, or of masculine strength, in every culture. A delicate neck is such a tempting trait that in some societies women's necks reach Alice-in-Wonderland extremes, as among the Padaung or Karen people of Burma, who stretch their cervical muscles with rattan and copper coils until their neck bones separate. Women all over the world wear clothing styles that put the neck on display. In

America, even hard-driving career women who wear formal suits resist buttoning their collars all the way up. As a feminizing trait the neck is too expressive to hide.

A man's neck is thicker, shorter, and generally brawnier than a woman's. The muscles are larger, the covering skin has little fat to mask the muscular cords, and the throat cartilage protrudes. The bulge in a man's throat, his prominent "Adam's apple," and the contrasting smoothness at the front of a woman's neck are not glaring sexual differences. But even minor contrasts like this would register if they were reversed.

A woman with a prominent voice box would seem a little less attractive, a little less feminine. Anyone casually looking at her might not be able to say what's "wrong" in so many words, but the subtle masculine cue would not go unnoticed. In the same way, a man might seem more boyish and less "rugged" without his bulge. It's a minor thing, but the visible smoothness would be just enough to alter the masculine gestalt. Cosmetic surgeons understand this. One of the final procedures in male to female sex-change surgery is shaving the throat cartilage to get the right feminine look.

The Shoulders. Few traits define gender with the yin-yang clarity of shoulders. Thanks to the growth-stimulating effect of testosterone, the male hormone, a man's shoulder girdle is stouter, its bones thicker, and its muscle mass heavier than a woman's.

Broad-beamed shoulders are on every woman's "most-liked" list. Their size and squareness convey the essence of strength without making force the bald issue it becomes when a man displays an overmuscled physique. Shoulders understate the power issue and telegraph virility without seeming to kick sand in a woman's face.

As signals, sturdy male shoulders send both visual and tactile messages. Wide shoulders give a man's body the basic wedge shape women like. But more important, women perceive broad shoulders as body parts they can touch and embrace. By laying her head on her man's firm shoulder a woman can feel secure.

Feminine shoulders are narrower and more delicate, but squareness is as appealing in women as it is in men. Thickness, measured from back to front, is the key gender contrast, not length as gauged across the shoulders from left to right. Narrow *and* wide shoulders appeal to a man's omniverous vision. Narrower, the shoulders suggest immaturity; wider, they make a waist look smaller and show up more when they're flexed, pitched, and rolled. Whether a woman's shoulders are tiny and sloped downward or as boomingly wide as Joan Crawford's, they strongly tempt the male eye with their gracile thinness and seductive range of movement.

Arms and Hands. The reason many men seem to eat up women's shoulders with their eyes is that nature included in their design two rounded orb signals, one erotic pearl on each side. A woman's upper arm, with its sinuous deltoid muscle and subcutaneous fatty "pillow," suggestively curves off the edge of her shoulder girdle. These fleshy, curvilinear hemispheres attract more notice than most men realize. In a sleeveless blouse, a woman's upper-arm bulge releases a primitive tactile response in a man, and he will find almost any excuse to reach his open hand out and cup the fleshy orb. This is particularly the case if her arm above the elbow is slim, because the narrower her arm, the more visible the orb sign.

Narrow feminine arms attract because they contrast with the thickness of masculine arms. As is the case with many gender signals, there's nothing *intrinsically* appealing in narrow as opposed to wide. Rather, the contrast itself, the identifying sexual difference thickness communicates, is what attracts. Men like women's wrists to be delicate, narrower than their own. They appreciate fingers that are thinner than their own digits. Women know this intuitively, of course, and wear fine bracelets to make the wrist contrast more' noticeable. Nail polish, too, not only lures the eyes to the hand but makes the fingers seem longer.

Gender contrast is the main message. Note that a man takes pride in his arm size, particularly in his biceps. The biceps muscle is rounded, has "friendly" connotations, and yet is also a visible index of strength. Developed, the upper arm has the same tactile appeal as a broad shoulder. Men should realize, however, that a little bit goes a long way in muscle-building. Yes, the biceps should show, but avoid overdeveloping them to the point of narcissism. Balloon biceps connote to a woman that a man is so into his own body that hers is secondary. For all but a small cult of women who appreciate bodybuilding as an art form, magnum, sculpted physiques of the Arnold Schwarzenegger genre aren't attractive in a courtship sense. Most women find overblown muscles vaguely repellent or even menacing.

Women prefer strong-looking hands and sinewy, "thongy," wrists to full-bodied beefcake builds. Men's hands and wrists have a unique visual, tactile, and personal appeal in the feminine world view. Being touched with a hand is psychic proof that a man is giving his full attention, that he is strong, yet sensitive and gentle. Compared with the hand's expressivity, defined triceps and *latissimus dorsi* seem uninteresting through the female lens.

Perhaps now is the time to explore masculine strength in its deeper aspects. Male strength is controversial in these days of feminist politics, and rightly so, but there's no getting past the fact that women still value a man's virility and "vital force" in courtship.

Strength has deep, tangled roots in the human mating dance. For 99 percent of our history on earth, people lived in small groups as hunters and gatherers. During these millions of years, men took the lead in hunting and in protecting the group from predators and outside enemies. Women cared for children and gathered something like three-quarters of the food supply. In the courtship arena there was competition among the men for mates. Once "married" (presumably the institution extends well back into prehistory) a man, using his strength, kept other men away from his mate (or mates). And as his political and economic fortunes rose, again partly as a result of his virility, so did hers. A woman had a stake in her man's physical vitality because he protected her and contributed to her status in the tribe.

Speculative, yes, but women today respond to male strength for the same reasons. Call it a primitive holdover if you will, an anachronism or a useless vestige from the past—but a modern woman never lists "timid," "soft," "weak," or "short" as attractive masculine traits.

Stature. To get an idea of just how primitive our courting criteria still are, consider shortness. "Short, dark, and handsome" won't soon be a household phrase. And the reasons are all irrational. Psychologically we still equate largeness with clout. It's cruel, but short men are subjected to height discrimination in courtship.

Shortness works effectively for women in boy-meets-girl, as it helps draw men through its infantile influence. Although many women are finding that smallness and cuteness don't wear well in the corporate world, in today's courtship short stature aids attractiveness as much as it did in Mae West's era.

Actually women can have it both ways. Both tallness and shortness attract. Indeed, many men prefer taller mates, as couples like Carlo Ponti and Sophia Loren, Mickey Rooney and Eva Gabor, Willie and Cynthia Shoemaker, and Nancy and Henry Kissinger show. Of course, it helps when the man compensates for his own shortness, as the above men do, with financial or political strength.

Tallness still confers an advantage on the male side. Being able to gaze down on a mate links into the primitive psychology of masculine strength and protection. We feel the power differential slide back and forth as we talk first to someone smaller, then to someone taller, than ourselves. You can experiment with that potent little visual angle—first wear clogs or cowboy boots, then thin sandals—and experience the amazing difference inches make in the pecking order. Most of the time you'll feel slightly "older" than smalls and "younger" than talls, without consciously realizing it.

I've seen men sit and talk to women for hours in singles' bars without getting up for fear of revealing their size. Because torso stature is more uniform—we carry our height, or lack of it, in our legs—people match up better in the seated position. But no short man needs to telegraph that he feels the height disadvantage. Short men can hold their heads erect, carry themselves proudly, and display a fireproof confidence that would make taller men seem insufferably arrogant. There's no need to be wimpish or scrappy just because you're small. A confident presentation will magnify the image others have of you.

The Chest. A man's chest is in head-to-head competition with his shoulders for basic "huggability." The masculine ribcage, with its larger volume and stronger pectoral development, has more of a basic "keg" symmetry than a woman's. A full, barrel-shaped chest gives a man a cuddly appearance and certain teddy-bear qualities thinner men lack. Big-torsoed men seem powerful, because their chests unconsciously call to mind the "puffing-out" display that is found in all vertebrates in situations of threat. Even preschool boys stand taller, raise their chins, and puff out their shallow ribcages to challenge other little boys. Animals from fish to mammals swell, inflate, bulk up, and fluff out to seem larger and more threatening.

That women like ample torsos helps explain the appeal of large-girthed men, such as TV's Ed Asner (a veritable sex symbol to some), professional football-player-turned-actor Merlin Olsen ("Father Murphy"), and TV journalist Charles Kuralt. Such men appeal in ways neither they nor women seem to grasp fully. What Ed Asner-like bodies lack in classical athletic leanness they make up for in hug potential and raw "cuddlability."

A woman's chest is shallower and less heavily muscled than a man's. But nature didn't let this strategic fleshy surface go to waste. Instead she decorated the terrain with two rather remarkable orb signals. Female bosoms enlarge after puberty as sexual signaling devices. Other primate females, chimps, for instance, have breasts that inflate only when they're milk-filled; if a mother ape isn't nursing, her breasts are flat. The only reason a woman's breasts are full-looking from sexual maturity onward is courtship communication.

Like other orb signals, bosoms excite a man's eyes while stimulating his tactile sense. But breasts also have the dubious distinction of being the most talked-about part of the female body. If the measure of an organ's importance is the number of "folk" words used to describe it, then the human mammary gland is prima donna.

American men, some say, have a breast fixation. Many North American men do indeed harbor a fascination that borders on the pathological, or goes beyond it, as the widely circulated skin magazine, *Jugs*, suggests. But male appreciation of the bosom transcends our own culture. Breasts are universally esteemed, and the same erotic standards apply everywhere.

Take New Guinea. In the Trobriand Islands, women don't cover their breasts, and Trobriand men critique them with a keen eye and a surprisingly technical vocabulary.

Nutaviya is the word island men use for full, round, firm breasts. *Nupipisiga* is the name for small, undeveloped, girlish breasts. Another term likens a flabby bosom to "hanging ripe fruit." Still another refers to sagging, wrinkled, aging breasts, and one graphic phrase compares thin breasts to the "aerial roots of the pandanus tree."

No, breasts aren't only an American totem. And around the world the male preference is the same. *Nutaviya*, medium to large, curvilinear, nonsagging breasts—such as those found for the most part in teenagers and women under twenty-five—are the standard. Because full bosoms communicate sexual maturity, gender contrast, tactile pleasure, mothering, and fertility, it's no wonder men read the signals and grow enthusiastic.

The Waist. Perhaps the most potent of all gender signals on the female body is the hourglass figure. Men everywhere froth at the mouth over narrow-waisted women. It's likely that the hourglass figure has dominated the beauty scene for the whole forty-thousand-year history of *Homosapiens*. And chances are good that the basic "cola-bottle" shape will still be irresistible ten thousand years from now.

Fashions come and go. Size standards fluctuate from decade to decade, from Mae West hefty to Lauren Hutton slim. But the narrow waist remains. Of course, it's a relative thing. The world's tiniest waistline, measuring just thirteen inches, belonged to Ethel Granger of Peterborough, England, who otherwise had a normal-size frame. The true meaning of "narrow" is thinner than the hips. Any woman with a waistline measuring approximately 15 percent smaller than the circumference of her hips has a valid hourglass shape, a waist capable of fibrillating the male heart.

Many women who haven't achieved the currently popular athletic, spare look assume that they aren't attractive. But it's just not so. Hyperthinness is only a fad, more a fashion than a true courtship signal. The hourglass shape itself is more important than slimness, and besides, the athletic shape excites fewer men than the mass media would have us believe. Given a choice, the average man will choose a voluptuous form over an athletic, boyish shape.

Of course, women who measure 31-31-31 or 40-40-40 do have a valid image problem. To whet a man's visual appetite they would need to alter their bodies' proportions to within the 15-percent tolerance. No woman needs a 36-26-36 figure, the beauty-contest ideal and a waist-hips differential of nearly 30 percent. In courtship, 35-30-35 is pleasing, as is 36-34-40.

The point is this. A woman needn't starve herself to fashion-model extremes to satisfy a man's visual appetite. Without too much effort she can achieve the "15-percent solution" and be *more* attractive in a courting sense than a slim-hipped mannequin.

But beware of the corollary point. With a waist equal in size to her hips, any woman who thinks men won't notice is only kidding herself. No optical illusion works. The male eye won't be fooled in the all-important matter of the hourglass figure.

There's some hard evolutionary logic at work here. Slim waists are innately attractive. It's as if a man has no choice. He likes thin waistlines because he comes from a long line of ancestral males who liked them, too. Millennia ago, men who preferred either prepubescent stick figures (of nine-to-eleven-year-olds) or Humpty Dumpty feed-sack figures (of already pregnant women or menopausal females) *fathered fewer children* than the men who were aroused by hourglass beauties. A thin waist combined with ample hips connotes (unconsciously) the simple ability to procreate. It is, finally and undeniably, *fertility* that is a woman's greatest courtship tool.

The Lower Limbs. Leg length is a sign of sexual maturity. As boys and girls reach puberty, their limbs lengthen proportionally to the size of their torsos. Thus long legs work as a beauty trait in men and women because they carry part of the contrast between child and adult. A man, with his vision bias, passionately admires mature feminine legs, and enjoys looking at the stretched limbs of models, pinups, and Las Vegas showgirls because their legs are "supernormally" long.

But short-legged women need not despair. Men find small legs just as attractive, but for different reasons. They may admire showgirl stature, but most men choose women *smaller* than themselves because cuteness—the small size once again connotes immaturity—still carries more weight in courtship than classical, long-stemmed beauty does. The name of the game is cuteness.

Watch men's eyes reflexively drop like stones to a woman's derriere at a business meeting when she walks to the front of the room to give her sales report. Even in serious settings, feminine hindquarters draw male eyes as candlelight draws moths. "Buns," with their fatty accumulations, are yet another brand of orb signal with the same visual-tactile appeal of the upper arms and breasts. It's hard for a man to talk about female behinds and not gesture with open palms.

When we began walking upright, our gluteus maximus changed position and gave us true seats. Monkeys and apes have flat, "seatless" posteriors, but when a female comes into heat her sexual skin may swell outrageously into a visual sign of readiness to mate. And to make sure males appreciate the swollen hindquarters, female apes and baboons "present" their rear ends for inspection. That is, they turn their behinds toward a male's face to solicit his interest.

Women's posteriors work in the same way, except that after the age of twelve or thirteen they are *continuously* swollen. The gender message is therefore constant. Women don't "present," unless you count certain disco steps, the cancan, and sitting on laps. That male and female derrieres contrast is more than clear to anyone who appreciates the root point of designer jeans, which is to make it possible for men and women to "present" their hindquarters even though they're fully clothed. Women's derrieres are larger, rounder, and fatter than men's. A firm female bottom projects, lifts, and separates more than a man's, and these are precisely the "shapely" features that drive a man into limbic tachycardia.

Women, too, appreciate rear ends, as Christie Jenkins makes clear in her book, *Buns: A Woman Looks at Men's*. A man's buttocks are the only real orb signs he possesses. Backsides are among the few male parts that seem truly "vulnerable." There's a lesson to be learned hearing women comment on seats tightly wrapped in professional football uniforms. When a woman calls the posteriors of the biggest, toughest men in America "cute," you know you're dealing with one potent signal. Male buns are less sexy, less erotic, that is, than they are merely soft and "friendly," and it's this unguarded, accessible quality that gives the masculine derriere its drawing power in courtship. Any man who neglects his orb signals reduces his chances.

Weight. Bodies grow steadily heavier with age. Weight gain throughout life is a cruel but firm statistical fact. As fatty tissue collects on waists, thighs, and legs, it unfairly gives shorter people a "stumpy" appearance. Instead of a sexually mature wedge shape or cola-bottle figure, many middle-age men and women present an image more like a Mason jar. In a poll that asked what men found unpleasing in women over the age of fifty, the number one liability was fat. Women were more forgiving of a man's body weight, but disliked overhanging bellies and sagging bottoms, too.

From art, history, psychiatry, and anthropology we know that the most important female signs are breasts, waists, and hindquarters, and the strongest male signs are the "wedge" shape (shoulders wider than waist), strong hands, and taller stature. Because nature has, in effect, programmed us to admire youthful, sexually mature bodies—bodies most likely to bear offspring—there's no denying the fact that dieting and exercise confer an advantage after age thirty. In courtship the benefit of staying in shape is understood in the current folk wisdom, but few middle-aged or older people truly appreciate how attractive they can be just by staying in reasonably good shape. Indeed, by mimicking the body signals of youth, older men and women can be highly competitive in courtship, almost unfairly so, when they combine physical attractiveness with the sexually alluring status of age.

Aroma Signals

The human body from the neck down is a veritable cornucopia of gender signals. Diagrammed, with all the sexually expressive territories drawn in and labeled, our bodies would have the gerrymandered look of a side of beef on a butcher's chart. But the body's eloquence doesn't end with touch and sight.

Like many animals, we broadcast sexual messages through the chemical medium of scent. Next to touch, in fact, smell is our most potent, primitive and "unreasonable" sense. Odors trigger powerful sexual moods, wholly outside conscious awareness. Aromas bypass the neocortex and travel directly to emotion centers in the limbic brain. Once known as the rhinencephalon, or "nose brain," the limbic system can detect certain odor cues without giving us the sensation of having smelled anything at all. Experiments show that scent traces too tiny to register consciously can change our blood pressure, respiration, and heart rate. Many scientists now suspect that we routinely read emotional scent cues from other people.

Men and women anoint themselves with sweet, spicy, or musky fragrances in nearly all societies. Micronesian women use the odor of flowers and pleasant-smelling fruits as attractants. American men wear Kouros, a scent combining herb, wood, moss, floral, and lavender tones, or Calvin, a fragrance with a light citrus smell. American women spray on perfumes advertisers describe with words like "untamed," "unbounded," "soft and warm," and "totally feminine." Ads for Estée Lauder insist that their perfumes give women "presence."

It's true. All life originally came from the sea. Down deep, where darkness reigned, smell was the key to finding food and mates. When life came to the land, smell continued to serve in the areas of eating and sex. So even the more exaggerated claims of perfume-ad writers are not far off the mark.

Sexual aromas do convey "presence" more personally and suggestively than visual signals do. The smell messages we exchange in courtship are 100 percent emotional. Our body's own aromas are truly "unbounded" as they waft in all directions through the open air. And because we can mask but not actually control our sexual odors, the word "untamed" fits. As for "warm and totally feminine," well, the olfactory signals released from a woman's scent glands can tell men when she's sexually excited.

As emotional temperatures rise, men and women give off different bouquets. Women have 75 percent more apocrine scent glands than men have. Apocrine scent, the gamy aroma we scrub and deodorize away, is both a gender identifier and a sexual lure. Apocrine sweat is not the clear, salty fluid that moistens our hands and dampens our armpits. Watery, cooling sweat, which does, however, help to spread the apocrine odor, comes from tiny reservoirs known as eccrine glands, found throughout the surface of the skin. Our apocrine glands—larger and more numerous, incidentally, than those of other animals—are concentrated in the navel, around the nipples, and in the anogenital region.

But the most massive accumulation of apocrine scent glands is in our underarms. Sexual arousal, anxiety, and threat stimulate the apocrine glands to secrete a pale fluid that the skin's chemistry quickly turns into "body odor." Underarm hair and eccrine sweat help aerate and broadcast the pungent message.

There's little doubt: scent increases the magnetism. "I'm coming to see you," Napoleon once wrote a woman. "Don't wash." The *Kama Sutra* says the perfect "lotus woman" has a highly attracting odor of musk in her sweat. In some tribal societies lovers exchange garments to keep a partner's smell with them. Many have heard the story of the Austrian peasant who easily seduced women he danced with after wiping their faces with a handkerchief he kept in his armpit. Casanova wrote about "something in the air" of his lovers' bedrooms, a balsamlike aroma so intimate a man might choose it over heaven itself.

Science has isolated an aromatic chemical from women's vaginas and has discovered that the same chemical found in female monkeys stimulates sexual behavior in males. Recently, a scent known as androsterone has been found in men's sweat. The same substance in boar saliva attracts sows, makes their ears wiggle and their eyes shine. Experiments tentatively suggest that androsterone, which women describe as a pleasing, musky odor, can make men seem more attractive and interesting.

Men who "sense" the aggressive air in locker rooms, weight rooms, and gyms may be responding to androsterone. Boars respond aggressively to the aroma. Experimenters sprayed Boar Mate, a cosmetic fragrance for men, on chairs and claimed that while men avoided the marked seats, women sat in them.

It's too early yet to know how powerful odor truly is in human courtship. We give off sexual scents, it is true, and after puberty boys and girls show a preference for heavier, muskier aromas over previously liked sweet and fruity odors. Many women like the "clean" smell of a man's body more than any covering colognes he may wear. Men like strong perfumes as well as a woman's natural odors.

Natural is the key to courtship aromas. The fragrance of the genital organs partly explains the increasing popularity of oral sex since the 1960s. Oral-genital stimulation occurs in animals as primitive as marsupials, who sometimes lick the genital areas in courtship.

Short of oral sex, however, the best courting strategy for both sexes involves more than a brisk scrubdown in the shower with deodorant soap. In a Fragrance Foundation survey, men and women rated odor an average of 8.4 on a scale of 10 as an important ingredient in sexual attraction.

After bathing, men should wear only enough aftershave or cologne to define an odor "signature" at close quarters, under twenty-four inches. Don't use smell as a long-distance attractant. Strong aromas on men are too direct and blatant, and they interfere with the body's own odor. Use a stick deodorant, not an antiperspirant, and not too heavily, so your underarms will release a small amount of their naturally adductive apocrine smell.

Women can send stronger odor signals with perfume because the male nose is less "observant" than the female's in these matters and needs a more powerful signal to get the message. He'll perceive your sweet "signature" smell from a greater distance, from several feet away, without blatancy getting in the way. A woman's stronger aroma doesn't put a man off, because he's already stimulated by the visual cues. The perfume just enhances the effect.

Women, too, can benefit by deodorizing their underarms

less than totally. With your perfume applied on the "pulse" points—wrists, knees, ears, temples, in the crook of the arm, above the heart, and on the neck (where heartbeat "warms" the scent)—and your apocrine glands left partly "on," you'll have the right olfactory aura for courtship.

The Artful Body

The human body is nothing less than a work of art in service to courtship. The earliest known sculptures, so-called "Venus" figurines dating from 25,000 to 22,000 B.C., celebrate the female body's curved shape. The most famous piece of all, the *Venus of Willendorf* from Austria, has great breasts and the swollen belly of a woman in late pregnancy. She has no face, just a knob for a head. Instead of an hourglass figure, Ms. Willendorf has the shape of a hurricane lamp.

Some see this as evidence that Upper Paleolithic men found grandscale obesity beautiful. But the early Venus figurines were fertility charms, not sex objects meant to stimulate masculine erotic juices. Not sex itself, but the *results* of sex, were depicted.

Two thousand years ago Venus returned to the classical world of Greece and Rome with a slimmer, nonpregnant form. Many still regard the ancient statues, such as the now-armless *Venus de Milo*, as models of perfection in female beauty. Look closely at these sculptures and you'll see overall bodily smoothness, thin necks, small breasts, sinuous shoulders, full hips, and narrow waists, constricted but not exactly thin. The classical Venus shape wouldn't win a modern beauty contest, but as a courtship shape it remains unrivaled. Any form that survives for more than two millennia as a prime standard of beauty deserves imitation. No woman needs the supernormal figure of a

Raquel Welch or a Lynda Carter to attract a man. You can achieve full potency with the more-natural Venus shape.

The exemplar of male beauty has to be Michelangelo's *David*. Michelangelo carved the best masculine traits into marble almost five hundred years ago, and nothing has changed. The first thing you see is the sinewy wrist and large, vein-backed hand curling onto his lower thigh. Then there's the visible biceps, definitely potent but not oversized. The wide shoulders, narrow waist, and "wedge" shape project strength without the slightest intimidation. David's neck is rather thick, a bit too wide, in fact, but the projecting Adam's apple and taut muscular cords are perfect. His abdominals show the right soft, rather than hard definition women like. He's on the tall side, standing sixteen feet high, but proportionally he's the quintessential male shape, lean and strong—but neither too lean nor too strong.

Sculpture and proportion are the keys to modern courtship, because in effect we sculpt ourselves with clothing. As we'll see, anyone can project the right Venus- or David-like shape with a little help from the tailor. Even the Black's Beach crowd spends most of their courting time in clothes.

Quiz

- In the "perfect courting outfit":
  - a. You wear three-color contrast.
  - b. Your top is darker than your bottom.
  - c. You wear a lemon-colored scarf or tie to bring out the yellow hues in your face.
- The best way to attract a preppie is to:
  - a. Dress like a punk rocker.
  - b. Dress like a Christian Jock.
  - c. Wear an Izod sport shirt, khaki pants, and Top-Siders. ®
- Clothes say both what you *are* and what you are *not*, so you must strategically show *both* sides of your personality. True or false?
- To attract a man, dress to stimulate his sense of touch. To attract a woman, dress to whet her visual appetite. True or false?
- The reason that high school boys wear tight jeans, loud-striped shirts, and "message" hair, while senior citizens wear baggy pants, olive-dull shirts, and dark-colored baseball caps is:
  - a. Annual income.
  - b. Political affiliation.
  - c. The requirements of boy-meets-girl.
- Clothing that is asymmetrical—a diagonal stripe, a blouse worn off one shoulder, an alligator appliqué worn on the left pocket—works to catch the eye. True or false?

8

Clothing—
Dress to Obsess

Every day she rides home on the 5:10 express from the university where she works as a librarian. Every day it's the same seat, halfway back on the right—and the same clothing style. The librarian's neutral-toned workaday outfit is a study in plainness. She has on a beige turtleneck sweater, a beige raincoat, beige slacks, and light-brown, sensible shoes with plain brown laces. For makeup she's got two stingy patches of blush on her beige face; she doesn't wear mascara, eyebrow pencil, or lipstick. There are BB-size gold earrings attached to her lobes. A short, wire-tight perm stuck on her head like a cap and thick glasses with putty-colored frames round out the picture. Even though she has a pleasing face and an hourglass figure, no man would court her. Beige Dewey decimal, sackcloth-and-ashes academic, her costume says, "Just pass me by."

And men do. It goes without saying that many men are less-than-attentive observers of how women dress. But at lower thought levels, down where he makes his courtship decisions, nothing escapes a man's notice. He "knows" when a woman dresses to be seen and when she dresses to hide, because her clothing speaks a language his limbic brain understands.

People began wearing clothes thousands of years ago chiefly to cover our genital organs. But dress quickly evolved beyond fig leaves and animal skins and, in an interesting twist of purpose, became a device to *display* our sexual traits. Nowadays tailored clothing can make men look taller, stronger, and more wedge-shaped. Modern women's clothes can embellish the all-powerful hourglass shape. Ideal courtship clothing extends the wearer's natural masculine or feminine powers.

It's hard to imagine what courting would be like *au naturel*. In a roomful of nudists, few people stand out. Faces, limbs, hair, nipples, blemishes, and a thousand moles move in a background of monotonous flesh. At a nude party, nothing really "grabs" your attention, and you begin to appreciate how lackluster our skin is compared with that of leopards, zebras, and brightly colored fish. Human flesh has a limited vocabulary and simply cannot titillate the eye the way a blazer with shiny brass buttons or a sequined blouse can.

Outside of a few members-only bars with adjoining orgy rooms, nude courtship is unheard of. No culture on Earth sets its mate-seekers naked on display in the village square. In fact, exactly the opposite happens. Men and women in all societies decorate their bodies during courtship. From Eskimos to Tahitians to the Bushmen of South Africa, the sexes ornament or dress up—distinctively—to attract each other. Unisex is not the costume of choice anywhere. Give Chinese lovers a choice, and the shapeless Mao suit would go the way of miniature "lotus" feet.

Most courtship clothing worn around the world is loud, let-out, colorful, and hog-stomping exuberant. The main message is "I am available." Designer jeans, Gucci loafers, striped polo shirts, wine-colored pullover sweaters, and fuchsia jackets worn over red-yellow-and-aqua blouses say, in effect, "Notice me, for I am courting." The librarian's low-profile beige outfit, on the other hand, seems to say, "What, me court?" Dress boils down to the contrast between, "See me," or, "Skip me."

Contrast lies at the heart of courtship communication. Shades of difference carry all the key sexual meanings in an outfit. Understand clothing's "grammar," understand, that is, how apparel signals contrast—appreciate the myriad different ways men and women festoon their bodies to attract one another (or to discourage advances)—and you'll never break courtship's unwritten adornment code. Feminine apparel looks, feels, and often even sounds different from masculine garb. When a woman wears a mauve skirt with deep pleats that swing and bracelets that softly chime with the rhythm of her steps, she stands in high contrast to the man in the Brooks Brothers suit.

Clothing shows both what a person *is* and *is not*. The most primal message is the contrast between "human" and "animal." Without her artistic body scars, a Bafia woman of Cameroon considers herself indistinguishable from a chimpanzee or a pig. Without her lip and gum tattoos, a Maori woman of New Zealand would think her white teeth and red mouth resembled the muzzle of a dog. We adorn ourselves because it's the human thing to do.

Another distinction conveyed by our dress is "we" versus "they." By strapping a board tightly on a baby's frontal bone, the Flathead Indians of the Pacific Northwest created the high foreheads they considered beautiful. The high-domed look also helped distinguish Flatheads from members of other tribes. Male versus female, rich versus poor, young versus old, homosexual versus heterosexual—contrast after contrast broadcasts from our clothing's rich store of signals. Punk rockers dress like punk rockers, Republicans dress like Republicans, and courtship follows strict clothing lines.

Tell It Like It Is (. . . or Isn't)

The best way to read clothing is to list the "is" and "isn't" messages in columns headed *Identity* ("I am") and *Disclaimer* ("I'm not"). Every courting outfit is a medley, as it were, of Is and Ain't.

On the Identity side is a person's basic "signature" display, the habitual baseline garb a man or woman *always* wears. Signature clothing signals set people off as distinct personalities, as individuals. In *The Catcher in the Rye*, Holden Caulfield always wore a red hunting cap. Albert Einstein's trademark was rumpled pants and electroflyaway hair. Katharine Hepburn wears trousers and keeps the front of her neck covered with a scarf. Humphrey Bogart wore a fedora and a wrinkled trenchcoat. Self-proclaimed "Doctor of Gonzo Journalism" Hunter Thompson (immortalized as "Duke" in the *Doonesbury* comic strip) wears Topsiders without socks and a scuba diver's watch and clamps a Rooseveltian cigarette holder in his teeth. The basic message of signature apparel is, "I am I."

No one comfortable with his own signature garb needs to change. But in the early stages of courtship it's good strategy to leave the stronger, off-putting elements at home. No-holds-barred shows of personality only intimidate prospective mates who don't yet know that obviously lovable creature, the "real you." Only after you're judged "safe" does the signature become likable. So in the beginning, wear shoes, cover up the tattoo, and leave your fright wig in its box.

Also in the I Am column are all those clothing messages that show social status and personal ties. People who dress alike affiliate, become psychic allies, because same is *safe*. When everyone at the garden party has on nubby crewneck sweaters and khaki pants, Izod golf shirts, and tasseled mocassins, you know you're deep in preppie country. The message is, "I'm a college-educated, career-oriented, upper-middle-class American." And in this milieu, any unknown person dressed in cowboy boots and jeans might not be an instant hit. The courter should dress in the style of the courtee.

It all changes once people get to know you, of course, but before the ice melts, clothing messages are important. They're taken seriously. Every adornment signal, from the soles of your shoes (thick neoprene, thin leather, elevator heel, flat heel, stiletto spike) to the angle of your hat brim (pulled down, pushed up, set horizontal, set cocky) will be interpreted as a *willful* message of what you are and are not, and of how you expect to be treated. A person will fall in line with your clothing's implicit expectations as if they were stenciled on the front of your tee shirt.

Play it safe when you don't know people, and dress like the natives—the Western folk, the country-club set, the Chamber of Commerce gang, whomever. Only the very famous, the Salvador Dali or Truman Capote types, can wear whatever they want, because fame makes their personalities known and therefore "safe."

Reveal Versus Conceal

The clothes you wear will either display or mask your neck, chest, waist, shoulders, and other secondary sexual traits. The world's most concealing costume is the full-length robe, shawl, and veil devout Moslem women wear to observe the custom of purdah. No skin shows, no shape shows, and a netted mask blots out the face. Only two sexual traits, stature and gait, are left to disclose femininity. And at the other extreme is the world's ultimate revealer, the colorful French string bikini—a costly version of that most ancient bit of female garb, the pubic apron—which leaves little to the imagination.

Few bodies are shapely enough for string bikinis, but fewer still deserve total masking. Since the Industrial Revolution, clothing has evolved so far beyond the constraints of bulky animal skins and rough homespun cloth that now, thanks to textile science and the discovery of certain optical illusions, every body can look sexier than it truly is. By strategically revealing some traits while concealing others, designers make it possible for all of us to look like winners.

On the male side, several strength illusions built into the contemporary business suit, which conceals everything except a man's neck, head, and hands, have made it a world-class "power uniform." A suit jacket accents the masculine wedge shape by making a man's shoulders seem thick and wide-beamed. And because the coat's hem drops nearly to his dangling fingertips, his upper body seems a third again as large as it really is. When the jacket is buttoned, the chest appears to have a truly massive surface area, and the angle of the lapels gives the male torso a flared-out, expanded, and puffed-up look. Finally, the colorful necktie directs the eyes upward to the craggy masculine head, perched like a fierce pumpkin on a granite slab.

The business suit covers a lot of skin, but subliminally accents a man's power traits and therefore his masculine sexuality. Since only his head is exposed, a man can bring the full force of his authority-connoting face to bear in business—or courtship. Even a soft, frail body looks more mighty in a form-fitting suit, so it's worth paying for the services of a skilled tailor. The average man will look better in a tailored suit than Burt Reynolds would in an unaltered one right off the rack.

Women's footwear exaggerates feminine sexuality, notably, the female walk. By adding inches, high-heeled shoes make a woman's legs look longer, and by causing her feet to flex, they throw her calves into high muscle tonus. Not only do high heels make her calves look thinner and more shapely in the process, but, by altering a woman's center of gravity—angling her hips and lower back to the rear, which makes necessary a compensating forward thrust of the ribcage—they change her whole way of walking. Wearing spiked heels makes a woman's hindquarters protrude, her breasts jut out, and her body bounce with every step. Even ordinary legs look lovelier in heels than shapely legs do in flats.

The most fascinating courtship outfits conceal *and* reveal body parts at the same time. Take the slit skirt. Any man will tell you that legs peeking out from behind tailored wool "curtains" are every bit as sexy as long, miniskirted shanks. It's partly the drama of repeated unveilings and partly the fact that draped legs appear and disappear so quickly that the male eye only has enough time to catch their most shapely *profile* lines. Women's legs are more sinuous and alluring seen from the side than from the front or back, and the repeated "quick shots" of the calf against the cloth backdrop afforded by slit skirts reveal the optimal curves.

That bare legs are less attractive than partly concealed ones is well known to manufacturers of nylon stockings and pantyhose. The skin-tight covering seems to lengthen and smooth the legs, as well as give them a softer texture and a subtle, glistening veneer. Stockings hide the bones and tendons of knees and make light-colored legs contrast less harshly with their surroundings. Thus, the leg's shapely edges, its curving silhouette, show up more; the ankle seems thinner, and its fleshy surface area seems smaller. It's easy to see why sheer stockings have survived for so long as courting devices.

Designer jeans also work on the conceal-and-reveal principle. Tight enough to emphasize the curves of hips and derriere, they also make your legs more conspicuous because denim colors contrast more with light backgrounds than naked flesh does. Legs look longer because designer trousers hang more loosely on the legs than does a snug-fitting stovepipe jean. White or gold top-stitching down the seams gives an onlooker's eye a long, uninterrupted line that reinforces the impression of length.

Ideally you'll be able to find a pair of designer jeans that fits. And "fit" is the watchword. Fit is what makes Normandee Rose and Sassy Chassi the potent courting signals they have become in the past five years. Also, the little insignia on the seat gives those near you permission to inspect your buttocks. The little label says, in effect, "Look here." Which is the main reason *not* to don hugging jeans unless your derriere is one of your top traits. Ironically, designer jeans will make even a slightly big seat look several sizes larger. Anybody who is not truthfully thin will court better in looser-fitting, pleated pants with straight legs to convey tallness. It's better to be honest in front of the full-length mirror, because when you walk out the door your jeans will tell it like it is.

The conceal-or-reveal concept works because it rests on the out-of-sight-out-of-mind principle. Child psychologist Jean Piaget discovered that children under nine months think a toy literally vanishes when it's covered with a napkin. A variant of this cognitive law also works in adults. Anyone who conceals, say, thick ankles or withered biceps or teacup ears need not worry about whether partners will think the concealing odd. Your true image is everything that *shows*. What's hidden is just not there.

Colorful Versus Drab

Unlike many animals, human beings have splendid color vision. Originally, seeing different hues helped us find brightly colored fruits, berries, nuts, and other wild foodstuffs. Much later, after our bodies lost their hairy coats, leaving us with little but drab flesh, courtship naturally adopted color as an eye-catcher, and in every society mate-seekers began using blazing tints. Courtship became a moveable feast of loud patterns and rainbow hues.

Skins of exotic animals probably served in the earliest outfits. After all, tiger stripes and leopard spots evolved over millions of years as attention-getting devices for mating. The vertebrate eye is highly attuned to lines—to borders, edges, frames, reticulations, and linear contrasts—and few designs draw the human eye as powerfully as animal stripes do. By wearing a zebra-skin vest or a tiger-skin cape—or a fabric printed with those markings—men and women can give off the same potent, feral courting messages nature spent so much time designing. The mind has no difficulty reading the spots and stripes of animal courtship, nor does it fail to understand the beastial sexual meanings.

For these reasons, stripes emanate from our courting garb. You see stripes everywhere—the blue-and-white rugby shirt, warm-up tops with white stripes running across the shoulders and down the arms, multicolored ties, striped crewneck sweaters, contrasting primary-red cummerbund sashes on black dresses, light-hued sweaters with vertical striping at the armholes, red- or blue- or black-on-white diagonally striped blouses, and so on—dominate the singles scene today, because nothing can stop an eye with the primal force of the old-fashioned striation. You will recognize the standouts at a party by their stripes.

"Something old, something piped, something bold, something striped" is good advice for anyone choosing courtship clothes. Bold primary-colored stripes attract attention even in a large crowd. But a percussion-striped top may be too loud to look at for an extended period. After five minutes of strident tomato-red-on-white, eye fatigue can set in. A person may find it uncomfortable to keep gazing at you. So it's helpful to mute the stripes by wearing a neutral-colored sweater over the shoulders or by bringing along an earth-toned overshirt to regulate the effect. After attracting notice and locking into a conversation you can put the sweater or shirt on and turn down the stridency. In effect, you can present two versions of yourself at one party.

But stripes and lines need not be loud to attract notice. So edge-conscious is the human eye that *any* contrast, any border or subtle trim will say, "Look here." A powder-blue top, dark denim jeans, and a soft-hued raspberry belt, for example, will attract attention without overloading the senses. As our eyes rove about a body they seek linear detail and come to rest on borders. Lines draw as much notice as colors.

Clothing is a roadmap for the eyes. You can plot the gaze routes and destinations with startling precision. In the case above, the raspberry-belted waist will bear the burden of being seen first. Then a man's eyes will move up or down, but will always return to the belt. A white-satin ribbon sewn on the hem of a periwinkle or lime dress will pull the eye downward, so the wearer's legs will be more noticeable. Light- or dark-colored shoes will have the same downward-pulling effect. The white "swoosh" patches on a man's dark-blue Nikes will bring the eye to his feet and encourage women to give his body a head-to-toe once-over as their lines of sight sweep up and down from face to shoes. Black-velvet spaghetti straps will make a woman's shoulders more prominent; men's eyes will return again and again to the contrast of the black against her flesh. By labeling your best features with lines, straps, bands, braids, ribbons, plaits, pipings, hems, sashes, scarves, lace, and filigree, you make sure they're seen.

Eyes will move to the lighter, brighter costume elements first, to white collars and cuffs, for instance; then on to skin, to the face and hands; and finally to the darker, duller parts of an outfit. Anyone dressed all in light tints—in a cream-colored sweater and an off-white skirt, say—will stand out, but not for long. Eyes quickly find noncontrasting clothes uninteresting and summarily strike the wearer from the vision net. But if the blanched-out person is psychically erased, anyone who dresses only in dark shades won't show up at all. The darker the outfit the farther away its wearer seems to be. A dark-gray outfit devoid of light contrast can swallow a person whole.

So if you must wear dark clothing, also wear light. If you wear a neutral beige or tan, also wear color. If you wear solids, also wear a print. Without contrast, hue, and lines one's personality will stand out like lumber. A fly on the wall will seem more interesting than drab, contrast-free clothing. Anyone who zips into a plain outfit vanishes from the courtship scene.

Everybody knows that colors carry emotional connotations. Red is exciting, yellow is lively, light blue is calm, dark blue is cold, maroon is quiet, orange is warm, rose is soft, lavender is rich, dark green is cheap, brown is wholesome, and purple is opulent. But no matter what your favorite color, you can't objectively judge what looks best on you. Because of eye color, hair color, the contrast between your hair and skin, and the texture, transparency, and orange-based hue of human skin, you can't easily know what to wear. On this score you need outside opinions.

After you know that, say, blue-green is your best color, you can begin designing maximum-strength courting outfits. Start with a blue-green shirt or blouse, which should pick up your eye color and complement your skin's basic hue. (Avoid any top that brings out yellow in your face.)

The simplest way to add contrast is with a neutral-colored bottom—khaki pants or a beige skirt, for example. To maximize visibility, make sure the top is several shades darker than the bottom, as this reverses the "natural" light-to-dark order you see as your eyes move from sky to earth. A dark color on top helps to grab attention.

If red, yellow, blue, and green suggest feelings, the amount of white or black a color contains—its lightness or darkness—will tell others how approachable you are. Overall, lighter colors welcome and darker shades forbid.

Let's start with the extremes, black and white. White almost universally connotes moral cleanliness, chastity, and purity. In most cultures pure white conveys "goodness." Anyone wearing white is psychologically less threatening, more easily met. We all like Snow White, and we trust Colonel Sanders enough to eat his chicken. White is the best-all-around color for a courtship top because of its brightness, high-contrast possibilities, and connotations of safeness and honesty. To keep the dark-on-top visibility, wear a jacket, sweater, or vest in your best color.

Pure black is serious, ascetic, unemotional, and "hard." Like a celestial black hole, the color won't let feelings escape from its total darkness. By withholding emotions, a black-leather jacket suggests mystery and gives its wearer an aura of "cool." Flat black is worn by studious co-eds, joyless academics, and persons in mourning because it hides all the passions of the color spectrum. Punk rockers might wear black to seem hard, to show the future is grim or to mourn the death of rock and roll. Whatever the reason, though, it's harder to be friendly with a stranger dressed in black, because the color gives away nothing that is personal. Black doesn't invite contact, unless the material is velvety or satiny, that is, tactile, or unless the wearer is so fair that the dark shade makes the blondeness monumental.

White is approachable, black less so. And the rule applies to the lightness and darkness of colors as well. A man in a powder-blue jacket will seem more sociable, other things being equal, than one wearing a navy-blue blazer. And the main difference is just the admixture of white to get the pastel tint versus the addition of black to get the navy.

Luckily, we can wear more than one color. A navy blazer, white shirt, and light-gray slacks are one classical and effective courting blend. Wearing three colors is optimal in courtship, because a viewer will find that level of color complexity more interesting than a single shade, and easier to "decode." When you know what your best color is (that is, the best hue for your face), choose two others to complement it for the "optimal-three" look.

Three is the magic number underpinning the design of the most eye-catching of all patterned fabrics—national flags. Fifty percent of the world's flags are tricolored, and 25 percent are two-colored. Only about 20 percent are four-colored, less than 5 percent use more than four colors, and no national flag is single-hued. Every country wants a strong, high-visibility banner, and through a natural process of selection half of all flags flying today sport three colors, many times incorporating horizontal or vertical stripes. (Although nations of the world avoid diagonal stripes because they connote instability, lines on the bias work exceptionally well on dresses and tops to grab attention, precisely because they do seem off balance.)

No one should dress like a flag, of course, but the principle of three-color contrast is too potent and tested to disregard. A single color is quickly boring, while four or more can overload the eye. Wear three contrasting hues that complement your skin color and your body's natural contrast.

"High-contrast" men and women, those with light skin and very dark hair, can wear bright colors and bold contrasts, black and white, dark blue and gold, and so on. People with light skin and fair hair, "low-contrast" people like Robert Redford and Shirley MacLaine, look better in light shades and muted contrasts. For instance, a low-contrast man with pale skin and sandy hair shouldn't wear a navy blazer, white dress shirt, and gold-and-blue tie, because the dark shades and stark contrasts would overpower his natural coloring. By the same token, a contrasty woman with creamy skin and cocoa hair would do well to avoid subdued color combinations of say, wheat, sand, natural, camel, and beige, because her own body tones would only make her clothes seem drab.

It's hard to overestimate color's importance in the mating ritual. Wearing a predominantly quiet, neutral outfit—one that is all white, all black, all gray, all beige, all brown, or all khaki—will get a flat, neutral, apathetic response from those nearby. Color "scripts" people, tells them how to proceed. Every courting outfit needs color signals that say, "Notice me."

A splash of brightness here and there is all it takes. All the librarian in beige needs is a contrasting orange belt, an orange scarf, and a light-catching, chunky-bead necklace. These color cues will put her in focus and create a magnetic mood toward which men will unwittingly gravitate. Color invites emotional participation.

In the courting arena it's good strategy to use one, sometimes two, neutral shades to get the optimal color contrast without appearing gaudy. To maximize femininity wear "warm" colors (red, orange, and yellow hues), all of which contrast strikingly with neutrals. Remember that vivid colors—bright reds, hot pinks and so on—seem to jump at viewers and create a sharp body outline. Intense hues are best worn in crowd conditions when you want to stand out and shine. In a roomier setting medium-intensity colors—clear hues without overpowering brilliance, like tropical blue, burgundy, turquoise, raspberry, and wine—are eye-catching and seem open and direct, neither dull nor shocking. By wearing the most vivid hue in the three-colored outfit on a scarf, belt, or ribbon, that is, on the smallest clothing piece, you can attract attention without overpowering the eye. A red sash on a black dress will attract as much notice as a black sash on a red skirt.

Because we associate masculinity with "cool" hues (blue, green, and maroon) and "earth tones" (rust, cinnamon, camel, chestnut, toast, elephant green, and so on), men dressing for courtship would do well to wear these colors as part of their three-part harmony. Again, let the tie or pocket square carry the brightest hue.

Your choice of courting colors will require compromises. Although more socially forbidding, dark shades like navy blue and charcoal make a man seem to "weigh" more and give him an air of authority. There's a psychic trade-off between friendliness and stature in colors like dark blue. Short men do better courting in darker outfits because the added authority offsets the cuteness of small stature. A woman feels easier breaking the ice with shorter-than-average men, and the high-status dark shades will lead her, subliminally, to take them more seriously in a conversation.

Strategically, the taller-than-average man should wear a submissive-looking pastel tint somewhere in his courting outfit. An effective costume for men in the six-foot range is a navy vee-neck sweater, a flat-pink shirt, and light-gray slacks. That style has it all: authority, three-color contrast, dark above light, soft texture—and pink.

Why pink? Pink is the "friendliest" color, the most submissive of all hues. Any pastel—powder blue, pale yellow, light green—any hue with white added liberally, is "meek." But studies of the color pink have shown it to be a virtual inhibitor of aggression. Put a violent prisoner in an all-pink room and within minutes he becomes physically weaker and psychologically sedated. If you're an outgoing person, a pink golf shirt will make your approaches less threatening. If you're an introvert, flat pink will make it easier for a woman to come up and talk.

Male Versus Female

Of all the messages radiating from courtship clothing, few
are more important than gender contrasts. ''Male'' or
''female'' must come through, because the success of an
outfit correlates directly with the number of masculine or
feminine signals it encodes. As sexual contrast increases
so does attractiveness. Without clothing signals to transmit
masculinity and femininity, you have a roomful of asexual
human units.

Every piece of clothing emits its own gender cues, even
hat brims. To look masculine and ''cool,'' for example,
men wear the brims of their baseball caps low over the
eyes. It's how Marlon Brando wore his cycle cap in *The
Wild Ones* and how Humphrey Bogart wore his fedora in
The Maltese Falcon. But flip a man's bill *up* and ''cool''
reduces to ''goofy.'' Leading men and tough movie charac-
ters always have their brims pulled down, but little boys,
comic-relief sidekicks, and village idiots—anyone to be
taken less seriously, like the foolish airplane mechanic in
Thirty Seconds over Tokyo—have their visors flipped up.
Panama, Stetson, and cowboy-hat brims are worn down by
most men; even sailor caps and berets are worn low on the
brow to show the ladies a rakish image. In contrast, older
men often wear their hats high on the forehead, an indica-
tion that they've abdicated their tough-guy role and bowed
out of the courting arena.

What explains this cue? A low brim does make a man
look stronger and more threatening. Threatening because,
pulled down, the visor seems to frown like an enormous
artificial eyebrow. And stronger because a low-riding hat
makes the eyes appear to be more deeply set. In effect, a
man's hat brim is a synthetic brow ridge, an embellishment of that bony trait's inherent masculinity.

Hats and caps are returning to the male fashion scene, and it's partly due to the appeal of brims. Harrison Ford helped bring the fedora back in *Raiders of the Lost Ark,* and Tom Selleck often wears a baseball cap. So don't leave headgear out of your collection of courting props.

For reasons of gender contrast, women's hats ride higher on the skull and show more forehead. Many feminine styles have no visors or brims at all. When a lady's hat does have a brim it tends to be flipped upward. Sun hats have large, floppy brims that curve down, but they don't have the threatening look of male visors. Women's hats work well in boy-meets-girl because they help frame the eyes and make the face look bigger relative to the whole head. The right hat makes the eyes, cheekbones, and lips seem to fill up the facial frame, a universal beauty trait shown dramatically in the face of Nancy Reagan.

Don't wear sunglasses indoors to seem mysterious and aloof. Shades are legitimately "cool," because they hide the emotional nuances of the eyes, but dark glasses telegraph coolness at a price. Because they sit so blatantly on the face they mark the wearer as something of a masker, an odd-lot character, which is not a bad thing in life but *is* detrimental in courtship. Eyes are too information-rich to disguise. People you may want to meet will think you're staring at them, and they won't look at you. Even lightly tinted glasses that interfere with eye clarity should be avoided if possible.

Courtship clothing should telegraph moods. In this regard note the pleasing effect of puffy sleeves. Few clothing inventions work better to convey femininity in courtship. The puffiness at the end of the shoulders you see in many dresses, blouses, and jackets is what is known as a "frozen gesture." Puffy sleeves mimic the natural raised-shoulder gestures women unconsciously use in wooing. Lifted shoulders convey submissiveness, so by *wearing* the gesture a woman makes it that much easier for men to come closer. The top with puffy sleeves—don't court without it.

Scoop-neck sweaters with puffy sleeves are more potent still. The rounded line of the scoop on your flesh will sweep eyes back and forth from puff to puff. And the soft, rich texture of the fluffy sweater radiates a persuasive tactile appeal that high-neck tunic tops lack. But the most eloquent top of all, the ultimate adductor, is the décolletage blouse worn entirely off the shoulders. Décolletage dresses delineate a visual frame above which female shoulders pitch, roll, and boil. The only reason breasts are sexier than shoulders is that the former are hidden. Unconsciously, men find shoulders every bit as erotic as bosoms. Flaunt them.

Shirring, fringe, pleats, and lace add an important tactile dimension to women's clothing. Ruffles and tuxedo-front blouses stimulate the male appetite for touch. A fragile see-through lace insert running down a sleeve, for instance, not only brings the eye to a woman's arms and emphasizes their length, but it can trigger tingling sensations in a man's fingertips at the thought of feeling the material and underlying flesh. Satins, suedes, and velvets give the same tactile effect without showing skin.

From a strict courting point of view—forget the madcap rules of "high fashion"—the feminine neck (the region from the lower jaw down to the top of the breast bone) is best left open to view. Don't cover the front of the neck. Left open its length and thinness clearly register. And necklaces do their best job when they lie on the bare skin itself. (Lines that decorate the flesh are more courtworthy than those on material, as the potent spaghetti strap attests.) The feminine neck is just too alluring to cover with a buttoned collar, a banded neck, or a turtleneck. Save these for home, school, or office, unless strategic reasons, "turkey gobbler" neck folds, for instance, dictate using them. A bared throat has as much seductive authority as a lowcut dress, and is a lot less blatant.

Men should wear collars. Leave them unbuttoned unless you wear a tie. It's not that a man's neck is unattractive and needs covering. Rather, collars make the male neck look thicker and less timid. A sturdy neck is a natural masculine trait, and clothing emphasizes the male-female contrast. Buttoned collars with neckties work to this end; but even without a tie a man should use his open collar as a frame to exaggerate the wideness of his cervical region. Any fashion that tries to deprive the courting male of a stand-up collar is doomed. Even if he wears a tee shirt, you'll see a man's jacket collar turned up. Every leading man in the history of film has his jacket collar standing at attention, because a turned-down collar makes a man look vulnerable. There's no need to flip your collar up in a singles' bar—it's a bit too dramatic for real life—but wearing a collar radiates your male image.

You won't see puffy sleeves in masculine garb, but shoulder pads, shoulder straps, and epaulets are as popular today as they were five hundred years ago. The military shoulder strap on a safari shirt doesn't add bulk, as suit-jacket pads do, but the bordering straight line helps make shoulders look bigger because of a little-known "framing effect."

Lines that run across the top of a man's shoulders or down the sides of his arms and legs—that is, the profile or silhouette—make his body seem bigger. Nature equips many of her larger mammals—bison, antelope, gazelles, and so on—with lines along the dorsal part of their backs to enclose them in a "frame." Framed, an animal looks bigger and closer when it turns its profile to bluff other animals with a "broadside display." The profiling stripes on military dress uniforms can make a man come on in courtship like a wildebeest, as it were. The frame is part of what women find attractive about "a man in uniform." A bush jacket worn over a dark sweater is good for courting.

Stripes on sports uniforms help to make football, baseball, and basketball players easier to see. But they also work to bluff the opposition with their optical illusion of greater size. It's little wonder then that athletic warm-up suits, frame-bordering ski sweaters, hooded rugby shirts, and other silhouette-enhancing tops are popular as male courting devices. Athletic garb can make a man seem vigorous and bigger. What's more, when he moves his arms so the sleeve stripes track across those on his chest, the lines seem to vibrate due to a phenomenon known as "edge-cutting." The visual flicker—not unlike what a female antelope sees when a male pronghorn's dark tail whips across the white patch on his rump—gives him high visibility.

For the same reason, visibility, women should wear jewelry as a wooing prop. Pins, rings, chains, pendants, necklaces, and so on show wealth, but their expense is less important than their visual effect. Jewelry's biggest job is to catch the eyes and bring them to the body. A pin worn on a blouse should have enough dazzle to draw the eyes to the torso and keep them coming back. Jewelry, with its glitter, gleam, and shine, is eye bait. A little sparkle goes a long way, though.

The Perfect Courting Suit

Women

Less is more. Resist the natural temptation to overdress. In the perfect courting outfit simplicity is the watchword, because the body's own signals must be allowed to show. Starting at the top, your hair should be long and fluffy. Soft hair attracts the male eye. Wear plain gold or silver earrings, highly polished but not too ornate, to pull a man's eyes back and forth across your face.

Be sure your neck and throat show. Put on a simple gold or silver chain or a strand of pearls. Or omit the necklace entirely; your neck is alluring to men just as it is. Take your rings and bracelets off. Bare your arms. Fingers, wrists, and arms already speak loudly enough.

Choose a top that is several shades darker than your pants or skirt, in a color that highlights your eyes. The top should have a scoop neck, not to reveal breast cleavage but to show the flesh of the upper chest. Your collar bones, or clavicles—indeed, all the slim bones of the female shoulder girdle—have a strong erotic appeal.

Regarding the shoulders themselves, of course they must show. But as sexy as décolletage is, you don't want an overstated, Carmen Miranda exotic look. So your blouse won't be worn totally off the shoulders. Rather, the straps will run across these expressive organs and cover a limited area between the orb signals of the upper arms and the points where the clavicles run into the top of the shoulder itself. This may seem a bit technical, to be sure, but the idea is to show the orbs and as much of the flesh and bony structure as possible without seeming too exhibitionistic. So a trade-off design, a strategic compromise, is called for.

What we're talking about is a nineteenth-century "bertha" style, now popularly known as a "peasant blouse," with a few modifications built in to bait the male eye. First, the fabric should not be cotton, but a downy, fleecy material like cashmere. A sweater has more tactile appeal than a blouse. Nothing works better to whet a man's sense of touch than a fuzzy, velvety surface. Even after millions of years of evolution men still like the feel of soft fur.

Trim the seductive top with a wide (3-inch), gathered ruffle that goes around your neckline and over your upper arms. Ruffles enhance the tactile pull and draw attention to the breasts in an understated way. The puffy overhang on the arms helps you achieve a dramatic peekaboo, or "curtain," effect men like, and also suggests the coy, lifted-shoulder "approach" signal.

Now, the bottom. If your waist is within the hourglass tolerance, accent it with a thin belt (which should show up against the sweater). If not, wear the top loose and unbelted. Thin-figured women look best in slim, but not skintight, designer jeans. For larger women a clingy skirt—pick one with a slit—is just right. Wear high heels and pantyhose with the skirt, platform shoes with jeans. And there you have it: a simple, adaptable courting costume that cuts through the layers of a man's resistance with one swift, powerful stroke.

Men

First you need a trim. Long, medium, or short hair, it doesn't matter—you don't want rogue strands, spiky tufts, or cowlicks grating on women you don't know well. Anything radically out of place early in the game is likely to annoy. So will a "too groomed," eager, car-salesman look. Get an artful cut, then muss it in a gentle breeze.

Women are close observers of detail. Whatever your image—prep, punk, jock, business, Baptist, beach bum, wildman, or regular guy—you must be well groomed. Clean nails, clean hair, clipped nostril hairs, and so on, are necessary because grooming has deep primate roots. The best-groomed monkeys and apes are always the most dominant, the ones who receive the lion's share of female attention. In the human mind, neat-and-clean still means high status.

Put on an expensive-looking flannel shirt. The color should be light. Camel is nice. The secret ingredient of your shirt is its rich-looking texture—touch is the way to a woman's heart.

Your top must have a standard collar for the conservative tone. Unbutton the first two buttons, and *only* the top two. Wear no chain, no rings, no pencil holder in the pocket— let nothing interfere with the shirt's soft appeal. Tuck the fleecy top into light-gray corduroy slacks, not western jeans, which wrinkle and draw the eyes to your legs and knees. With its tactile appeal, corduroy works best to stimulate the female imagination.

Don't buy skinny-legged pants. You want to convey an image of tree-trunk solidity when you stand. Unless you are six feet or above, don't wear shoes that contrast with your trousers, because conspicuous shoes will make you look shorter. The seat of your pants should be slightly snug to reveal the friendly contour of your bottom. (Avoid overly snug as well as baggy-seated slacks.)

The crucial part of the perfect male outfit is its "teddy-bear" overtop. Invest most of your courting budget in a soft, bulky-knit lambswool cardigan sweater, darker in color than your pants and shirt. The idea is simply this: make your appeal directly to a woman's keen sense of touch. Flood her brain with tactile cues.

Your cardigan should have leather-covered or horn buttons, which are more tactile than plastic ones. Leave the sweater unbuttoned so it contrasts with the lighter shirt. Make sure the "teddy-bear" top drops several inches below your hips to enhance the size of your torso. And it must have monumental texture—deep ribbing, patch pockets, ribbed cuffs, shawl collar to frame your head—which will speak a calm but compelling message: "Hug me."

With this outfit your shoulders will seem larger. The thick sleeves will convey the "idea" of biceps without that muscle actually intruding. Your hands will contrast with the arm cuffs and seem large; pull the sleeves up a few inches to show your wrists.

And that's all there is to it. You can substitute velour for the flannel, or a friendly tweed jacket for the cardigan. The idea is to seem warm, soft, large, and huggable. Avoid the Formica-hard image of shiny leather jackets. Don't wear loud satin shirts or all-dark outfits, and don't undo more than the two top buttons.

Remember, you're dressing for courtship, not for church, school, or a job interview. You're not trying to show status, wealth, political savvy, or fashion consciousness— just sex appeal. And not sex appeal in the blatant sense of big muscles and hairy chests. In courtship the motto is not dress to suppress, but: "Dress to Obsess."

Quiz

- It's good practice for a man to approach a woman from an oblique angle, that is, from the side, rather than head-on. True or false?
- A woman knows her face is looming too close for comfort when he:
    a. Turns his face away.
    b. Shows his tongue.
    c. Covers his mouth with his hands.
- In deciding where to take your date for dinner, you should consider the interior "mood" of a restaurant more carefully than its menu. True or false?
- The quickest way for a woman to get to know a man is to:
    a. Dance with him.
    b. Take him boating.
    c. Go for a ride together in a car.
- The most congenial nightspots offer:
    a. Music with a beat.
    b. Fluorescent lighting.
    c. Themes from the "safe past."
    d. Waiters instead of waitresses.
- All things considered, a lunch date can be as romantic as a dinner date. True or false?

177

9

Spaces, Places, and Interiors

The place is dignified by the doer's deed.
—*SHAKESPEARE*

One must follow circumstances, use the forces about us, do in a word what we find to do.
——*ANATOLE FRANCE*

From your window table amid the ornate, pastel décor of Les Saisons, you can see the sparkling big-city lights of Dallas, and you have to agree: Les Saisons definitely has it. Twenty minutes from downtown Atlanta, at The Hedgerose-Heights Inn, feasting on rich Continental food in an apricot-and-pale-green dining room trimmed with colorful sprays of flowers, you'll again perceive: The Hedgerose has it. Tantalizing foreign menus, soft lights, elegant furnishings . . . it all adds up to the same ineffable "thing": Romance.

Space can speak. The physical setting against which courtship takes place can help or hinder couples in ways far more subtle than they can fully grasp. And although roses and violins do engender in some of us a magical, romantic mood, the "right place at the right time" can turn out to be anything from a smoke-filled corner taproom to the backseat of a Dodge.

Making Time in Space

Whether couples meet in fake Irish bars, at McDonald's, in a bus, on a beach, or at a Baptist picnic, the first problem on their agenda is coping with the limiting dimensions of social space. The human person does not just stop at skin level. An invisible envelope of "personal distance" encircles each one of us, and only certain select "safe folks" are permitted through.

Personal Distance

Anthropologists have discovered a clear envelope that surrounds our body like a bubble. Known as "personal distance," this transparent sheath has a concentric, layered structure, something like that of a sliced egg. The inner nucleus, the "intimate" zone, zero-to-eighteen inches from the skin outward, is reserved for our most familiar contacts with close family, friends, and lovers. The next ring, the "personal" zone, eighteen-to-forty-eight inches in front of us, is used for dealings with more casual friends and acquaintances. And surrounding this is the "social-consultative" zone, which extends from four-to-ten feet in front of our bodies. Anything beyond ten feet, the "public" zone, is for our most impersonal interactions, such as lectures, courtroom testimony, stage performances, and so on.

Any man who violates these implicit North American body distances in courtship, any man who, say, moves his face into a woman's intimate zone without permission, is likely to feel her spatial barrier "thicken" as she pulls back, turns her head away, stiffens her shoulders, and compresses her lips. Seeing these defensive cues, he should withdraw from the intimate ring to the less-volatile personal zone.

The body's territorial bubble varies in size from society to society. A Britisher's space envelope is larger than an American's. An Arab's is smaller. Therefore a Texas woman may feel uncomfortable talking with a Saudi man whose face looms six inches in front of hers, and in turn he may feel snubbed as she keeps backing up to get out of his narrower personal zone. Bubble size is inconstant across cultures, but in every group the zones extend farther in front than they do out from the sides or behind the back.

Because the bubble balloons out wider in front, it's better to approach someone new from the *side*. Experiments show that head-on advances are the most unsettling. One study found that college students had sweatier palms—one telltale sign of anxiety—when approached from the front than when advanced upon from the rear.

Like the body, personal space has different shapes for men and women. A man will automatically have negative feelings about people who sit *opposite* him—across a table, say—than for strangers who sit down *beside* him. But for a woman the pattern is reversed. Sitting opposite her, an unfamiliar man across a table is not an immediate turn-off. It's the fellow coming up from the left who makes her wary. In libraries, men arrange books and papers and open briefcases as barriers against face-to-face invasions, but women line up their belongings to guard against encroachments from the side.

Understand the contours of individual space and you can approach an unfamiliar man or woman strategically. The best policy is to take the least threatening route. Seeing a blue-suited man with a gray beard sitting by himself in the hospital coffee shop, a woman should approach from his right (the dominant right side of right-handed people is less easily "threatened" than the weaker left side). Walking unhurriedly, without looking at him, she should place her tray on the table and sit *beside* him, about four feet away, right on the fringe of his personal zone. On the other hand, if this bearded man were approaching the woman, he would succeed best if he sat down across from her, a couple of feet to her right or left.

What the newcomer should look for to see if she is welcome or not is a telltale sign in the man's eyes. Mr. Blue Suit, the original occupant of the table, is in a deep psychological sense that space's "owner." It takes two or three minutes for a sense of sharing and equality to jell between the owner and the "invader." And for about five minutes Blue Suit will have the edge in deciding whether to start a conversation. So strong is the sense of territory and the power advantage it grants, that his eyes will exercise gatekeeper rights. He can look but she can't, because one perk of spatial ownership is a steadier gaze. You can look out your own living room window at people on the sidewalk, but when they peer into your parlor, it's felt as a threat. If the first inhabitant of a table looks back at a newcomer a *second time*, that's the signal that it's OK to open a conversation.

In courtship, locking eye to eye with a man or woman in effect "collapses" the intervening distance. Holding someone's eyes across a room is like bringing that individual right into your personal space. But as you do move physically closer, the amount of time spent in mutual eye contact shortens. Distance and eye contact substitute for each other. So from only four feet away, a locking gaze will bring a couple into rather uneasy intimacy. And within the eighteen-to-forty-eight-inch personal zone, eye-to-eye contact lasting longer than two seconds can be an unwelcome invasion of privacy.

In a conversation the patterns change. But as in certain other areas of courtship, every inch counts. The psychic gulf between friend and foe, between liking and disliking, and between warm and cool is usually evident in a precise three-inch margin. People who like each other, for instance, position their faces an average of three inches closer than mere acquaintances do. Measured nose to nose, most people stand nearer when talking to women (21½ inches) than to men (24½ inches). People the same age stand closer (24 inches) than when one member is older (27 inches). Acquaintances stand nearer (24 inches) than strangers (27 inches). The magic number is three.

In the crucible of courtship, therefore, success or failure often depends on inches. Standing just three inches too far away would subtly convey an aloof, indifferent attitude. But violating the twenty-seven-inch stranger limit, that is, moving inside the twenty-four-inch acquaintance zone, could make you seem to come on too strongly.

But you needn't carry a tape measure. Most people have an intuitive feeling for personal distance, its layers and restrictions. They unconsciously understand the structure of social space and stay in bounds. But less insightful men—women, it seems, have fewer problems in this area—often find the limits of personal distance frustrating.

All anyone handicapped with problems of personal-distance communication need do is cultivate a sensitivity to crowding cues. People unwittingly warn you when you've come too close too soon. If a woman feels crowded she will avert her gaze to one side and keep her eyes turned away. A man will angle his upper body left or right and lean away. Approached by a stranger, crowded within two feet, both men and women will cross their arms over their chests and take a small step backward. Lips compress, tongues show, heads turn, bodies squirm, and hands reach back behind the head. But all a "crowder" has to do is recognize the cues and pull back, just a little, and the "crowdee" recovers.

Stomping Grounds and Cruise Spots

The importance of space goes deeper than personal distance and body zones. Indeed, courtship is truly territorial in the biological sense, with fixed property lines and defended borders. It's not by accident that we call a man's hometown his "stomping ground." And when we say a woman "rules her roost," we're talking bona fide territory.

In a way, territory is to courtship what a field is to football—the space in which the game is played. You can play catch without ever stepping on a football field, but serious competition always takes place within the boundaries of a gridiron. Similarly, you can flirt anywhere, but winning a mate means pitting yourself against the local rivals on their own turf.

You can feel the competition and sense the larger territorial imperative of courtship in America on a Friday or Saturday night at the local teen "cruise spot." Every town has a place where its teenagers drive en masse to strut, stomp, flaunt, puff up, and display. In San Diego, the main courting ground used to be the asphalt parking lot of Oscar's Drive-In. That frenzied spot drew the county's high-school boys and girls in such numbers that the police were always having to close Oscar's down. That today, twenty years later, the restaurant is still a popular cruise site demonstrates just how fixed a courting territory can be.

The teenage cruise mentality is not restricted to human beings. You find the same phenomenon in insects, birds, fish, frogs, and in other mammals, in what biologists call *leks*. A lek, in essence, is a territorial show spot. The males of a species gather in one small area to attract females from the surrounding countryside. Only after the latter show up do real competition and the serious male displays begin.

Inside the lek—the same leks are used year after year for courting—males put on dramatic, eye-catching, ear-drawing snap-crackle-and-pop displays, while the females wander about and survey the field. For example, Lechwe waterbucks in Central Africa court in circular leks, a third of a mile across. Fifty to one hundred bulls prance or stand in exaggerated, head-held-high poses with their tails wagging and their penises erect. Cows entering the space set the males off chasing one another, fighting, and posturing with their lyre-shaped horns.

No one has seriously studied a human lek, as far as I know, until now. I admit feeling conspicuous hiding behind aviator glasses in a '70 Maverick, spying on teenagers at a popular cruise spot in Seattle known as Golden Gardens. I was the only person over thirty-five parked in either of the two rows of cars facing one another grille to grille across an asphalt "line of scrimmage." But I had serious anthropology to do, so I set a bottle of Lone Star on the dash, pulled down my cap, and took notes.

With the cars lined up on either side, full of quick-eyed, hooting, beer-drinking minors, the cruise line was like a gauntlet. Boys rode through in black Camaros, bodies bouncing around inside like monkeys on an electrified grid. A Ford pickup drove off the lot into a sandy field and spun "doughnuts," throwing up a small tornado of dust and divots. Girls in twos and threes ran the gauntlet in hotwaxed Toyotas and Pintos, their anxious faces held rigidly straight ahead, and returned again and again, making a circuit. Overall, it was a good example of swaggering, shrieking, varoom-varoom courtship, teen style.

Courtship, space, and male aggression fuse in one primordial nut. It's all out in the open in teenage mating rituals. So many hormones pump through a young adult's veins that wooing is bound to be on the wild side. Golden

Gardens officially closes at sunset, but so strong is the lek instinct—the need to swarm seems to increase after dark— that a police patrol car has to shut the park down every night with a bullhorn. After adolescence, boy-meets-girl moves into more sedate settings—country clubs, office parties, shopping malls, and so on—where territoriality is less obvious. But like the invisible Coriolus force, the compulsions of space influence our courting habits throughout life.

Courting Places

The lek principle is not as obvious in adult courtship, but it's still there. The grown-up mating game takes place in territories where sexual pairing is less obviously the main concern. A lot of postadolescent courtship takes place in "night spots," where men and women can eat or drink or dance or be entertained, or do all four, after dark. Courting has gone commercial.

"Night-spot" courtship is so popular that many restaurants and cocktail lounges now compete with more than longer happy hours or fuller menus—they also provide "romantic ambience." Which is to say, they package and market perfect courting spaces. Recent graduates of the nation's restaurant-and-hotel-management schools are now in the business of helping us woo.

Sensory Manipulation

So come on into the Milton Hotel's Ambience Room. Just freshen up in the entryway and relax. The manager has a firm grasp of group psychology and a swell plan for you. Push ahead into the subdued light filtering through the bar space, past the crowd, toward the illuminated area in the very back of the room. The splash of yellow light on the back wall is there to pull you in and guide you through. Design psychologists know that when you enter a darkened area you reflexively slacken your pace and quiet down. You get the same awed, reverential feeling you experience walking into a cathedral or a dimly lit theater.

Subdued lighting, they know, will make the crowd easier to bear. In darker settings you can get physically nearer to people, because personal space shrinks when the lights go down low. Notice that men and women bring their faces closer together when they talk in the bar's dimmer reaches. Intimacy goes up after eight when the management dampens the rheostat.

Candlelight from the crystal globe on the table makes faces look younger and softer than they look in bright sun. And the flickering glow casts a soothing, hypnotic spell that makes sitting with others, eyeball to eyeball, easier, because a glance at the dancing flame calms the nerves. Bathed in candlelight's peculiar influence, men and women take more time eating, converse more leisurely, and spend more time looking at one another.

Luminescence, glitter, sparkle, shimmer, flash, all the dancing pencil beams of light you see in the Ambience Room, work to titillate the eye. Bar owners spend thousands of dollars on spots, beveled mirrors, cut-glassware, crystal chandeliers, and sometimes even lasers, to create dazzling images with light. And the special effects have a subtle influence on mood. A "halo" effect sets in: people around you seem livelier and better-looking, more radiant, more festive—which is to say, more romantic—because the glitter rubs off.

Anthropologists will tell you that as darkness falls, people in tribal societies quiet down and huddle around the campfire. Nighttime brings its own special intimacy. As the group stares into burning embers and listens to the hissing logs, the mood becomes hushed, protective, and familiar. We've always had a special feeling for the hearth, and any bar or restaurant shrewd enough to install a fireplace, like the brick-lined one you see in the Ambience Room, helps even skittish people feel homey, relaxed, and secure. Few props comfort the human spirit or bring people together like a wood fire.

Fire psychology explains why the Ambience Room's golden tints arouse pleasant, happy feelings in us. Fire and yellow light come from the same end of the color spectrum. Yellow's link with bright sunlight also connotes airiness, brightness, and refreshment to most people. Advertisers use yellow's mood-altering effects to suggest achievement and modernity, and to make packages look bigger. It's not hard to understand how dining together in this gilt-hued room amid polished brass and soft-glowing gaslights can lead men and women to feel warm and tender with one another.

Color schemes affect courtship more than most of us imagine. Consider red, the most arousing of all hues. Red signifies fire and heat, as well as vitality, strength, and emotional excitement. Red may influence sexual appetites. Mice and birds change their mating routines when scientists bathe them in crimson light. Human interiors that are illuminated with lightbulbs that give off predominantly red light seem to have a more-arousing ambience than spaces lit with yellow-green and violet rays.

No one succeeds in the hotel-and-restaurant-management game without a thorough understanding of music. Music cuts through bar space like an apple slicer. Whatever the melody, whatever the volume, and whatever the lyrics, the first thing you'll respond to is the beat. There's a constant throbbing rhythm in a bar, like a heartbeat. Your brain, your partner's brain, every brain in the place, phases into one omnipotent beat. Suddenly everybody's moving, thinking, even breathing, together, causing synchrony (which usually doesn't kick in until the Conversation Phase) to occur earlier, in the Attention Phase. Getting to synchrony is what bar music is all about.

Whether the music is fast and invigorating or slow and relaxing, most bars play songs set to words. If subliminal advertising teaches us anything, it's that the unconscious part of our brain absorbs messages like a sponge. No matter how ridiculous the lyrics may seem when read aloud from a songbook, put to music the words seem "meaningful." The melody carries a phrase past our rational neocortex (right through the gullible hemisphere) to the emotional limbic brain, which can relate without hesitation or embarrassment to the gushiest romantic suggestion.

A bar's sound system puts out a constant high wind of suggestive love songs. Two hours of "Hot Blooded," "Ring My Bell," "Baby, Don't Get Hooked on Me," "I Want You, I Need You," and "Lovin', Touchin', Squeezin' " will put the most hard-hearted person in a courting mood.

Themes

Anyone who has been to San Francisco's Ghirardelli Square, Boston's Faneuil Hall, or a modern shopping mall has experienced the subliminal effects of "themed space." The theme concept was born in the early '50s in California, on "Main Street" at Disneyland. Disney engineers created a Victorian theme and a unified architecture in which nothing upset the harmonious Gay Nineties motif. Strolling through Main Street, you see no revolving gas-station signs or blinking neon advertisements for "adult books." There's no peeling paint or pigeon droppings, no panhandlers to put your subconscious on alert. The buildings themselves are scaled down, smaller than life. Everything on Main Street is reassuring, nothing is out of place, and therefore, in a deep sense, all is well.

The park's tranquilizing theme architecture—the same

spatial planning that has kept millions from running amok in the crowds that move through Disneyland's Main Street bottleneck on route to Fantasyland, Adventureland, and Tomorrowland—is now built into the design of shopping malls, restaurants, and hotels. Human-factors engineers know that harmonious, themed spaces can calm people and slow their pace. This in turn will make them more likely to spend time—and money—in the space.

The same thing happens in a singles' bar. Consider-Jake O'Shaughnessey's in Seattle, one of those Irish-themed establishments that caters to the urbane crowd. Jake's has a spacious standup area in front, adjacent to the bar, and heavy wooden chairs and marble-topped tables in the back. It's an easy place to meet people; the crush of bodies in the standup crowd makes intimacy unavoidable because there aren't any physical barriers. Jake O'Shaughnessey's is not an authentic Irish bar. But sometimes, with the Guinness beer on tap, the hardwood floors, the ceiling fans, and the barmaids in their turf-green velvet outfits, that fact is hard to remember.

Jake's is as American as Disneyland, baseball, hotdogs, and Mom's pie. So is Shakey's, with its framed photos of steam locomotives and Model T Fords, and its imitation gas lights. So is the Mad Hatter in New York, with its odd-lot hats tacked on the ceiling and sawdust on the floor. The active ingredient in all these themes is nostalgia, the "safe past." In a Captain Kidd, Old West, Roaring '20s, or Gangster '30s interior, you step out of the convulsing present into the "good old days." Because the props remove you from the here and now, courtship is that much easier. A modern service-station theme with dummy pumps, traffic cones, waiters in greasy uniforms, and a salad bar on a hoist would not exactly lead patrons to relax, talk, and spend money. Maybe in two hundred years people will court in a renovated Shell station, but right now that theme would be too close to home.

The contemporary singles' bar is designed with *old-fashioned* romance in mind. "Ve have vays of *making* you court," the faceless managers will admit, but nobody questions the manipulation.

Few people really understand how congenial the controlled atmosphere is to closeness. It's not the same as church picnics, husking bees, and ice-cream socials, because in a modern courting space people often pair before they really know each other. The singles' bar is a good place to court, but all who enter should beware. Themes and sensory manipulation can speed the process and collapse all five phases into an evening.

Singles' Bar Space

Nothing in a true singles' bar is left to chance, but the control is subtle. Many establishments feature "visual" drinks, strong but without any alcoholic taste. Frothy vodka or rum froufrou creations like the piña colada are popular because, unlike serious bourbon-and-7s, they seem harmless and softcore, and set a drinker off as being young and trendy, no matter what the true age. Strawberry or banana daiquiris in large goblets create a festive ice-cream-parlor atmosphere where drinking is OK.

The staff sets the tone for the whole bar. Management hires clean-cut young men for bartenders and wholesome, outgoing young women with girl-next-door smiles as cocktail waitresses. Bartenders dress in old-fashioned, 1890s barbershop-quartet outfits to seem psychologically less threatening, but the strong male presence behind the bar is still an effective reminder for drinkers to stay in line.

Because the single men pay for most of the drinks, restaurant-management graduates thoughtfully provide grinning, good-looking women to serve the drinks and take the money. Sound psychology, because the innate male courting hostility that cocktail *waiters* would set up could discourage many men from coming back. As it is, a man feels powerful without the competition, and gets to flirt with the waitress each time he buys a beer.

Women serve, but men fetch. That is, a man will go to the bar to bring his companion a napkin or another drink. This puts him in the convenient role of provider, with its obligating force. In many ways the singles' bar has a male bias.

The masculine undercurrent also shows in the "clubby" atmosphere of the singles' bar, with its dark wood, brass rails, and pictures of race horses, sailboats, and moustachioed early-1900s football teams. The underlying idea of the club theme is that if a bar can attract men, by catering to masculine tastes, the women will follow. Fewer men would go to a feminine-themed space to court. Besides, that reversal would run against the lek principle.

Of course, certain female amenities must be worked in to make the barroom attractive to women. The usual trick is to add little netted candlelamps, hang up some healthy-looking ferns, and put restrooms, coatracks, and full-length mirrors in the entryway. The idea is to eliminate those last-minute insecurities—to make it possible for women to groom before entering the lek.

The interior space itself promotes mixing and close contact. It's hard not to brush a few knees and derrieres as you move through the singles' bar's purposely narrow layout. You can't help but touch. The people standing elbow to elbow along the high tables expect it. Standing around is OK, too. If a person had to sit at a stool and buy a drink, three-quarters of the crowd would have to leave. But it's a known fact that many singles prefer to stand, because that way they're more mobile and the space is less "structured."

A word of caution: don't order a schooner of ordinary tap beer. Most singles' bars won't even stock draft because the management wants to discourage the surly "tavern crowd" from bringing in their own brand of adventure. And if the outfit your waitress has on seems a little reined in, an ankle-length dress with a button-up collar, well, that's just another way of keeping out the rowdy element, the rougher men who would only come in to ogle, get down, and raise the ambient adrenaline level to dangerous levels. The barmaid is dressed so she won't bring in ruffians and she won't compete with the single women.

Many singles' bars feature dancing. Dance is to humans what "bill-fencing" is to the albatross—a repetitive courting movement that links through synch. Dance is a world-wide form of courtship communication. It works whether you actually hold your partner or just stand apart and jump up and down together. Isopraxism connects men and women whether they embrace and rock slowly to the music or gyrate without touching around a Mexican hat. The principle of dance is simply this: the couple that moves together grooves together.

Take a minute and observe certain rogue movements on the singles'-bar dance floor. If the steps seem a little frantic, it's because the high speed accelerates courtship. The more movements a couple shares, the closer the pair comes to feel. Slow dancing, fox-trotting torso to torso, is fine for all the mated pairs on "The Lawrence Welk Show." But earlier in the mating progression, you'll see hot-blooded couples churning themselves into butter at the same savage pace jungle natives dance to in their "primitive" courting rituals.

Primitive is the operative term for all the wild movements of the mating dance. You'll see legs and arms reaching, pelvic girdles thrusting, heads bobbing, and shoulders twirling like windmills wherever you go. In New Guinea or New York, the moves attract attention and suggest the sexual act at the same time. Men and women smile, bounce, and sway through all three dimensions at once—reel, spin, squat, flap, tap, hip, butt, and bunny one another while they beat the air with their fists.

It's imperative that a person go out on the dance floor. If you can't dance just imitate the movements. Anything will do—the point is to synchronize with your partner, not look like Gene Kelly or Ann Miller. As an expressive tool, dance is too powerful not to use. It can catapult you directly to Phase Four, and by moving together for several minutes you'll feel a burgeoning togetherness, because few human activities are better suited to the bonding process.

Auto, Home, and Other Settings

Next time someone else drives, take a minute to feel the "total stimulation" of an automobile ride. We've become so habituated to the car experience that it's easy to disregard Detroit's influence in courtship. But more wooing goes on in the front seat than ever went on in the back.

Cars might be the best courting spaces available, especially for people who are not yet on intimate terms. Riding up front with a man or woman leads you both to commune on many sensory levels at once. As you sit just an elbow's length away, contained in a space no larger than a pup tent, the physical and psychic closeness registers right away. If a courting conversation is ever to flourish, it will do so in a moving automobile.

En route in a car, speaking is always easier. The normal gazing patterns don't apply. Less eye-to-eye contact is possible when the driver is watching the road, so the stress level diminishes in an automobile cockpit. Besides, there's so much to look at as your eyes gulp the onrushing view that normal gaze is unnecessary.

The steady hum, the hypnotic sense of motion, and the drawn-out togetherness are heady stuff to the brain's courting centers. With the couple locked off from the rest of the world in a private, carpeted, upholstered compartment, a drive in the countryside is not the casual date one might suppose. The seductive interior can put people on intimate terms in a hurry. One hour in a car together, booming down the highway with the tapedeck on, counts for more than a month of ordinary picnicking or partying.

Boats

Equally seductive are boats. Canoes, sailboats, speedboats, and Venetian gondolas are romantic because they rock. Board a sailboat and the ordinary laws of gravity are suspended. A small boat moves in three planes—up and down, front and back, and side to side—at the same time. Because a boat rolls, tilts, and undulates with every swell, and gives us an erotic sense of freedom, many people, especially women, report becoming sexually aroused while floating free on bodies of water. To take the person with whom you're reaching Phase Three on a boat ride is a powerful step forward.

What's more, just being on the water is psychologically comforting to many people. Our eye enjoys the glitter of sun and moon on the dappled surface, as well as the sky-blue color of the water itself (a shade that connotes peace, security, and contentment). Our visual sense is also innately comforted by "horizon scenes," open expanses where nothing in the space disturbs our ever-watchful line of sight. On a boat in calm waters or onboard a bouncing river raft, two people can feel close, free, and aroused. It's no accident that the Tunnel of Love is a water ride.

At Home

Visiting someone in a house, apartment, or trailer—in the "core home territory"—has several predictable effects on courtship. Our sense of home is strong, and no matter how humble the core may be, its inhabitants will feel more relaxed, self-assured, and in control there than in anyone else's territory. This means that a woman will have a power advantage in her own space. Visiting a man's apartment would make it harder for her to call the shots because there *he* would have the edge.

It's the same in the animal kingdom. The farther an animal strays from the center of its home range the weaker it becomes. A terrier may rule its backyard domain wolfishly, and greet trespassers with bared teeth, but five blocks from home is a different scene. The power gradient shifts and the tables turn; out of its exclusive bailiwick the dog will flee from poodles half its size.

Part of what makes a terrier omnipotent on its own turf is the way the dog marks its inner territory. The animal's secured core—that most-defended area around its master's back door—is "scent marked." Which is to say, the pet leaves smell images of itself on and around the porch to declare, "Mine." In effect, the family dog spreads out its personality to intimidate invaders, and marks the steps, railings, and azalea bushes with its own urine scent.

People also spread their personalities thickly on the floors and walls of their living spaces. Pictures, baskets, vases, photographs, curtains, and knick-knacks—everything a person hangs up, lays down, and sets around the new apartment only hours after moving in to "claim" the room—are more than just decorations. Every item, novelty, and conversation piece marks the territory. The visual display fills the space, sets its boundaries, and signals ownership to outsiders.

When you court someone in your own home, therefore, you risk overloading that person with wall-to-wall messages about yourself. At visit's end, the partner will have such strong feelings about you, one way or the other, that he or she will either want to return or never come back. Because of this you are much more likely to succeed on an early date if you set it up to take place *away* from home, on neutral ground. If you invite someone out to a restaurant rather than serving dinner at your place, you eliminate the turn-off potential of the unfair advantage, the greater power base, that operating in your own territory gives. Early in the game a date isn't ready for that much undiluted You.

Once you get to the final stages of courtship, going home is OK. Around the world, home is not merely a shelter against the elements, but a secluded space that insulates a person against too much visual exposure. Home, in other words, is a place to hide. Staying too long exposed to other's eyes is psychologically stressful, anthropologists have found, and people in every culture have ways to partition themselves off from view. Inviting an eligible sexual partner home is a universal sign of burgeoning courtship, therefore, because you're secluding yourselves from prying eyes.

When you get home do not proceed immediately to either the living room sofa or the bedroom—go someplace "safe." Go to the kitchen. The kitchen is the lightest, brightest space in most people's homes. With its shiny appliances, bright-toned counters, and stainless-steel surfaces it is a cheery, tactile setting, permeated throughout by the psychology of food. Sharing something to eat in this very nonthreatening, wholesome setting will help the two of you to connect in an unpressured and relaxed fashion.

Knowing you were coming, the host or hostess will have cleaned house, "groomed the space" in effect, to make the home core seem high status. In the animal kingdom, ranking males and females are always the best-groomed members of the group. The farther down the totem pole you go, the more scruffy an animal becomes. Of all the rooms precleaned for home courtship, none is more scrubbed than the bathroom. Personal grooming is crucial if a couple is to move to Phase Four—the general rule is that no one makes love with anyone who is less clean than him- or herself—so bathroom signals can be as damaging as soiled skin. Clean hands, clean mind, clean bathroom—take your pick.

If all goes well you will wind up together in the most secluded room in the home space, the bedroom, our psychic inner sanctum. Of course, a bed provides a perfect soft surface for Phase Five, but reasons for making love on sleeping platforms go a bit deeper. The bedroom is that part of the private space that is ultrasecluded, a hyperdefended spot where others are least likely to disturb the mating tryst. It's also the most personal area, the primordial nest, as it were, even though in American homes bedrooms tend to be sparsely decorated. Never invite a person in to see the etchings above your bed until you've laid the groundwork in the rest of the house.

Your Place in Space

Two objects cannot be in the same place at the same time, physicists will tell you. But occupying virtually the same space simultaneously is courtship's literal end and its main goal. Sir T. Herbert was right when he wrote, in 1634, "They become whole and frolicke, in small space."

The Spanish have the perfect word for it, *la querencia*. In this era of punk, funk, fake themes, and sensory manipulation, the concept still applies. *La querencia* is an inviolable, secure place, sort of a home. Technically, it's a special spot in a bull ring where the bull feels safe. Bullfighters know they should never mess with the bull in its *querencia*.

The concept of *la querencia* has never been applied to courtship, as far as I know, possibly because the term is archaic. Nevertheless, it's useful to think not just about the *person* you're near but about his or her *querencia* as well. Everyone has a sweet spot, of sorts, a "key distance" and a "right setting" where things are best. Unlike the example of the bull, whose sweet spot should be avoided, in boy-meets-girl it is precisely in the *querencia* where courtship works best. Sense the personal distance, study the setting and heed the silent dimensions of social space.

Quiz

- When introduced to a man, a woman should:
    - a. Turn so her body faces his torso directly.
    - b. Gaze at his face for three full seconds.
    - c. Lean slightly toward him.
- You automatically add points to your courting persona when you:
    - a. Take your hand away from your mouth.
    - b. Quit biting your lower lip.
    - c. Put on your best "serious" face.
- Most men prefer women who act like:
    - a. Jacqueline Kennedy Onassis.
    - b. Sally Field.
    - c. Charo.
- Most women prefer men who act like:
    - a. Charles Bronson.
    - b. Robert Redford.
    - c. James Bond.
- The macho guise is less a man-to-woman thing than it is a form of man-to-man bluff. True or false?
- Men like women who:
    - a. Present meek, dependent images.
    - b. Put on strong, seductive displays.
    - c. Show "spunk."

10

How to Be a Woman—
How to Be a Man

She was not beautiful but it took her only about ten seconds to persuade people that she was.

—*F. SCOTT FITZGERALD*

There are but three classes of men, the retrograde, the stationary, and the progressive.

—*JOHANN CASPAR*

It's not haughty cheekbones, full lips, or warm eyes. These features can't hurt, of course, but they're expendable. And it's neither square shoulders nor expensive clothing nor sparkling jewelry nor tallness nor doll's wrists. These traits play important roles in boy-meets-girl, too, but compared to demeanor—stance, carriage, mood, and poise—they're all dispensable. The single most important thing in courtship is how you carry yourself, that is, how you *act*.

Boiled down, the juice of courtship is behavior. A man's masculine bearing attracts, and a woman's feminine charms captivate. All else is secondary, as the following true case reported by Ginger Jones in a recent *Cosmopolitan* article shows:

"Bob" and "Janice," writes Jones, met in a jetliner on a Washington-to-Boston flight. There was no magnetic first glance across an aisle, no cautious reading of gender signals, and no flirtatious exchange of gestures. All Bob remembers about the first meeting is the sound of Janice's voice and the pleasant conversation they had. Janice recalls Bob's unruly silver-and-dark hair, his self-assured posture ("he knew who he was and where he was going")—and his blue eyes, thick glasses, and white cane. Bob was blind.

The combination of his self-assurance and friendliness on the plane—Bob asked Janice if he could stow anything for her in the overhead compartment as she took a seat in his row—helped set the stage a week later for a sailing date. Bob had sailed for years before his blindness and had little difficulty doing it now, with sighted companions to guide him.

Sailing enhanced the romantic mood. The gentle undulating movement on the water, the physical closeness in the cockpit, and the cooperation required to sail upriver moved them toward intimacy. In his nautical element, Bob had opportunities to show off his skill and ability to captain the boat. But just as attractive to Janice as his masculine, "take-charge" attitude—and his attentiveness to her needs—was Bob's willingness to let *her* pilot the craft without feeling threatened when she was in control. She'd noticed the same confidence before they'd boarded the jet to Boston, when he took a flight steward's arm to be guided through the gate. No brittle signs of defensiveness showed; Bob's self-assurance had stayed intact.

On the sailboat, courtship quickly advanced. They talked, shared food, swam together—and although Janice was a self-proclaimed "four" instead of a "ten," although Bob couldn't see her face, although Janice didn't have male eye signals to read, although Bob had no head-tosses, shoulder-shrugs, or batting eyelashes to guide him, although the list of deficits went on in ways most of us will never understand, their courtship resulted in marriage.

Masculinity and femininity carried the day, not just physical attractiveness. It was how they *acted,* not how they looked. By combining confidence, vulnerability, and a caring attitude, Bob avoided both the macho and the whimpering-mouse extremes. And by caring for Bob and being attentive without trying to take charge and mother him—as other women with fancier clothing and better figures had tried, unsuccessfully, to do—Janice avoided both the smothering and the vampish extremes. They played their parts well.

Masculinity

What do women like best about how men act? Over and over again Robert Redford came up when I asked this question. And it wasn't Redford's rugged, boyish, blond good looks women talked about, but his behavior. You can't deny his visual charm, of course, but women quickly moved beyond the surface to Redford's ''presence,'' the way he ''holds himself.'' Pin a woman down, dig to the roots of her feminine feelings for this popular sex symbol, and she'll say something like, ''Well, sure, he's great-looking, but he's also strong and sensitive, and he shows he's interested in people with his gestures . . . and the sensitivity, along with the confidence, really *draws me in.*''

Redford's air of confidence and sensitivity is what puts him head-and-shoulders above men who are merely handsome. In fact, ask women to decide between ''nice-looking'' and ''sensitive and confident,'' and most will choose the latter, hands-down. Serious-and-sensitive is exactly the combination of traits that made Robert Redford so magnetic alongside Jane Fonda in *The Electric Horseman.* As one woman told me, ''His every movement counted. He seemed to be without insecurities. He was sensitive to issues . . . I don't know . . . he just seemed to walk a fine line between vulnerable and macho.''

That's what women like. Strong and huggable. Men on the most-attractive list act something like Robert Redford. They don't do a lot of nervous gesturing, self-clasping, hand-wringing, fast talking, unnecessary moving about, or anxious introspecting, as Woody Allen does in *Annie Hall*. The men most appealing to women are animated but not jerky or nervous. They don't snarl or act tough or aloof, and they don't cruelly glare, growl, or beat on the table as Clint Eastwood does in *Magnum Force*. Redford-genre men neither go into shaky fits around women nor ignore them, Charles Bronson-like, with icy, macho ''cool.''

Macho Extremes

Virility—the masculine pose—evolved purely for reasons of courtship. By sending clear ''strength'' signals, men stand a better chance of attracting women. It's partly because the male power cues themselves convey vitality and connote protectiveness. Women admire white-knight traits in a man. But the major advantage masculine signals have is in the ongoing, junglelike, dog-eat-dog competition *among men*.

Men do battle with one another to win female attention. All masculine power struggles reduce to sexual displays. It's a less-visible brand of competition than you see between two red-eyed bull elk in rutting season, but the principle is the same: power displayed for sexual ends. Two male elk lock horns not so much to hurt or maim each other but to lure females. Butting horns is a test of strength and a form of bluff, but not a deadly struggle. Bull elks won't kill each other for sex. Head-butting has ''gentle-manly'' rules—you don't see a bull attack from the opponent's vulnerable backside or flanks, where he could inflict lethal puncture wounds, as bulls sometimes do battling mountain lions and bears. Rather, in their courtship battles, bull elk align head to head and smash antler against antler. There's less wear and tear, and the crashing spectacle in the pines draws female interest.

On the human courting ground, it's basically the same. A boss "lords it over" his men, swaggers, bluffs, rants, and raves—coolly ignores the opposition and rewards the loyal allies with kind words and a benevolent hand on the shoulder—he gestures to display his status and control. And in the process Mr. Big feels sexually superior to the rank and file. Women are more solicitous toward him, and it just happens that their attention has an obvious courting flavor. Women orient more to the Boss, smile at him, flex, tilt, laugh more, and so on, to keep on his good side. They court him; it's part of surviving.

If you've ever wondered why little boys constantly challenge each other to games of marbles, yo-yo contests, and foot races, now you know: courtship. They're testing their competitive wings. The battles get fiercer as adolescence comes on, and you'll find some boys literally cracking heads and shattering one another's bones on the football field. That's clearly a courting signal, because the football-hero mentality is still alive, if not quite well, in America.

Reduce any dangerous sport to basics and the bedrock motivation is head-butting. Don Gay, the Professional Rodeo Cowboy Association's World Champion Bull Rider, summed it up when he admitted that most men take up bull-riding to pick up girls.

Men lift weights, wrestle, and box for the same reasons Siamese fighting fish fan-out their red-and-black fins, open their mouths, and strike at fellow fighting-fish males: courtship. Eskimos butt heads; Yanomamo Indians stage vicious chest-pounding and side-slapping duels. With all the ritual blows, sometimes it's no fun being a man.

So deep-rooted is the power display that, to survive,

many men take masculinity to the limit. When a man's power signals get out of hand, when strength emanates without compensating sensitivity, we have what is known as the *macho guise*. The most extreme macho men in America belong to outlaw motorcycle clubs like the Gypsy Jokers, Satin's Slaves, and Hell's Angels. But some men just *wear* biker's clothes—a black leather cap with the visor pulled down onto aviator glasses, a Fu Manchu mustache, a black, sleeveless undershirt, a tattoo, a black leather bracelet with flashing silver studs, boots with heavy heels, dirty Levis jeans, and a black wallet clipped to a beltloop on a chrome chain. It's a man's way of telling you his horns are poised and he's ready to butt heads.

Macho is greatly misunderstood. Even men dressed in severe motorcycle garb can be gentle with their womenfolk. At least they don't treat females with the same buzz-saw intensity they do men. Just as the bull elk won't lower his horns and charge a cow, few macho men dress to over-power their women. The whole point of manliness, even of macho masculinity gone berserk, is to inhibit *other men*.

A Hell's Angel wears his "colors" for the same reason an IBM executive wears his three-piece suit, to survive in the power structure. Although motorcycle macho looks meaner on the outside than IBM reserve, life in either group can be a war of nerves and a steely test of masculine endurance. It's follow the leader, whatever the club. A lone male, peripheral and unallied, has a harder time winning mates, because a man is only as strong as he is in his group.

We've come a long way from Neanderthal and Cro-Magnon, but modern men still compete to rise in the status hierarchy. Now it increasingly takes talent, skill, and brains. But the necessity for strength in one form or another is with us still.

In courtship, macho rarely works when a man turns his

brute strength on a woman. Aimed in that direction, the tough-guy, knuckle-walker approach is at cross-purposes with itself. Never mind the motion-picture folklore which would have us believe that certain abusive, unfeeling men like James Bond are attractive. A little macho goes a long way.

The Right Balance

Here are some basic dos and don'ts for men who may be confused about the masculine role in these times of expanding feminine consciousness and women's liberation.

First, women are right. Hardcore, insensitive, macho poses are out. It's hard to believe women ever fell for the caveman approach. Indeed, it's debatable whether marriage by capture even existed. All animals court before mating—males and females exchange signals of harmlessness—and it's likely our primitive ancestors traded gentle, aggression-disclaiming signals, too.

Second, women are wrong. The radical theoreticians who forecast a progressive convergence of the sexes, who see men and women gradually behaving alike, who predict androgyny, that is, are incorrect. As long as we live in a competitive world where strength confers an advantage, power will survive for good or ill. The truth is, women like masculine behavior, and to be manly is OK. Just as long as sensitivity also shows.

So, go ahead and swagger a bit—but not *too* much. The stiff walk is an ancient male signal found in monkeys, apes, coyotes, bears, and other animals. Chimpanzee males swagger in courtship, stand up, and sway rhythmically from one foot to another with their arms held away from the body. Male gorillas strut to show off and hold their bodies stiff with the arms bent outward at the elbow to make themselves seem bigger and stronger. Men unwittingly stand taller, lift their chins, square their shoulders, and suck in their bellies around one another in locker rooms, poolrooms, and bars. Many men swagger and thrust out their chests at parties. Holding the upper body stiff automatically makes it roll more from side to side with each step. Teenage boys exaggerate the swagger in each other's company, but all men straighten themselves up to some extent in courtship. Women should forgive men their John Wayne walks and interpret the strut as an amusing bluff signal, not as a threat directed at them.

Women admire a certain amount of vigor, bluster, and showing-off, as long as it's man to man. The strong handshake, the firm pat on the back, the loud greeting, and the confident smile are positive signs showing that a man is making it in the male domain. Most women tolerantly understand that such demonstrative signals are necessary. Demonstative signals, also found in many animals, combine threat against other males with courtship of females. They do double duty, as it were. When a man conspicuously "pops" a match into flame to light a woman's cigarette, he's responding to an ancient courting pattern. Men can't help feeling a little more macho around each other when women are present. Add a good-looking woman to a group of fun-loving good ol' boys and they'll soon be at each other's throats.

The bluster usually flows man to man. Anybody who takes a demonstrative approach with women directly—any man who shouts, pounds the table, dominates the conversation, laughs too loud at his own rude jokes—and expects women to admire his manliness is bound to go home alone. Men should combine pinches of bluster with heaping tablespoons of sensitivity around women.

Men might try the following signals: Face to face with a woman, speak slowly. Tilt your head to one side and nod as she makes her points, to show you're listening. Lean forward, align your shoulders with hers, hold your face tipped down slightly toward the floor, Redford style, and gaze upward into her eyes from under your eyebrows. Look for three seconds at a time, then drop your gaze to the table for three seconds before meeting her eyes again. Don't turn your head away to the side; keep it still as you listen.

Pause one or two seconds before replying, for dramatic impact and to convey your interest in her and her ideas without either suggesting dominance or hinting at impatience. Go ahead and pinch the skin at the front of your neck if you feel like it, or clasp your hands on the table in front of you. These are submissive signals—you'd never see John Wayne clasp himself—but they also show sensitivity. It's natural to cup the chin when you're in deep thought; doing so will tell her you're genuinely thinking about what she said. Don't squirm, fidget, or pick at yourself, and don't cover your mouth with a hand. Keep your body motions to a minimum; remember that Jack Lemmon agitated is less attractive than Paul Newman calm. Self-control shows in measured gestures. It's the difference between Glen Campbell bouncy and Willie Nelson cool.

But don't carry sensitivity too far. Any man willing to dive into emotional trenches with women at the drop of a hat, like Alan Alda, who gives the impression of being overeager to plumb the depths of his own weaknesses and spill his guts in confessional conversations, is slightly suspect. Women admire the honesty, but miss the steely masculine essence, the wilder, Tarzan quality that brings on feminine palpitations, blushing, glazed eyes, and weak knees. Sensitivity is fine as long as it stops short of weakness. When, after some honest talk, a man says, "To hell with it, let's go out and have some fun!"—well, that's the semitough Burt Reynolds attitude women still like.

Don't be fooled when a woman calls a man who opens a door for her a chauvinist pig. That's political, an understandable overreaction to male domination in the business and social worlds. Feminism has come of age and softened a bit—Betty Friedan's book *The Second Stage* is a sign of the thaw—and women are freer to admit to conflicting feelings of independence and dependence. They want strength, support, good manners, flattery, and humor. In a word, women want balance.

Femininity

What do men like? Although they spend a lot of time talking to one another about women's bodies, dig down below the surface of a man's visual appetites to the hard behavioral roots of attraction and the same name comes up time after time. Ask, ''Who would you like to *spend time* with?'' and the name is routinely the same. You won't hear men answer Miss America or Catherine Deneuve or Marie Osmond or Sophia Loren or Christie Brinkley or Raquel Welch or any other totem-beautiful singer, actress, or model.

The most all-around desirable woman is—Sally Field. But of course: Field has all the standard beauty traits that crank up a man's sexual barometer. Still, what men admire most is the way she acts—they respond to Sally Field's vitality, to her spirit and indomitableness—that is, to her *spunk*. In the roles she has played, Sally Field comes across, more than any other actress, as a woman who plainly enjoys and understands men.

Coming at you off a movie screen, Field gives the impression that she grasps masculine psychology and its inner truths. She knows that men are deeply monogamous creatures, on the whole, so the fierce loyalty she displays in a relationship is appealing. Sally Field also knows that the masculine guise is a stone bluff. She can absorb muzzle-velocity macho displays and laugh, because she understands that what's really at the core of macho is a soft, vulnerable pocket of pulpy male ego. Sally Field women, it is clear, will love a man and nurture him without smothering him in dependency. Sure, Field-like females break down, just as men do, but give them warm attention and they mend, usually right away. Behind every pout a smile waits to break through.

Men like Sally Field's fleshy, "little-girl" smile and wide-open gaze. When she tilts her head, oscillates her shoulders, and stands close, her femininity and loyal, "puppy-dog" aura strongly radiate. Field moves around a lot—she gestures, fidgets, and shifts her weight, and her body covers a lot of territory in an evening. In a word, she's alive, and she energetically fills the space about a man. If she were to stand still, in one place, without gesturing, men might find her too reserved or too aloof for their tastes. As it is, Field is both engaging and personal. Men like her because she's feminine, vulnerable, and faithful—and she's got that ineffable steely stuff: spunk.

Women on a man's "most-liked" list nearly always have Sally Field traits. They aren't afraid to be feminine. Yet they don't overdo meekness or dependency. You won't see the Jacqueline Onassis finishing-school posture, arms hanging limply at the sides and a plastic smile that hides . . . who knows what? You'll see passion, but neither Ann-Margret nor Brigitte Bardot sex-kitten poses. Which is to say, you won't see gummy dependency or vamp displays. Overdone femininity is as damaging to a woman's courting image as macho is to a man's.

Femina and Dependa Extremes

Betty Yorburg points out in her book *Sexual Identity* that more women than men are passive, dependent, nurturing, verbal, and friendly. More men than women are power-oriented, physically aggressive, and emotionally inarticulate.

The sexes are behavioral complements of each other. But neither men nor women can truly know how the opposite sex feels without somehow looking through their eyes. Luckily, a few people have lived as a man *and* as a woman; they have seen the world through both genders' lenses.

Transsexual Jan (previously James) Morris has enjoyed both the male and the female world views. In her book *Conundrum* Morris reveals that *everything*—all aspects of existence, all moments of the day, all responses, all contacts—are different for men and women. As the hormone pills he took for eight years slowly changed him, as he lost his body hair, his rough male skin, and masculine muscles and gradually metamorphosed into a woman, James Morris, who had been a soldier, explorer, and mountain climber, a man's man, as it were, began seeing through feminine eyes. And the world looked different.

As a female, Jan Morris looked back on her masculinity as a kind of invisible "resilience," a protective yet emotionally deadening shield against the outside world. Without this blunting layer she felt physically freer but more exposed, as if she had no "armor." The feminine Morris experienced heat, cold, wind, sunshine, and moonlight more "physically" than before. She felt closer to animals and to flowers, felt less introspective but more self-contained, and grew more emotional. Colors seemed brighter, details became more interesting than the "grand sweep," and as a woman she saw things in themselves as important, apart from their cross-references to everything else. Jan cried easily and responded more to flattery than James ever did.

"Femininity" as a biological principle actually predates women. Femaleness, in fact, has an evolutionary past millions of years older than Homo sapiens itself. The emotional sensitivity, the nurturing attitude, and the gentle rather than forceful world view evolved in order to encourage mothering and infant care. The best way to understand

the female principle, and its male counterpart, is in terms
of contrast. C. S. Lewis remarked that femininity is to
masculinity as melody is to beat, or as an opened palm is to
a fist.

But men and women act quite alike in one area. Both
sexes often take their courting identities to the extreme
edge. Feminine signals easily get just as out of hand as the
exaggerated masculine signals, and the macho extreme is
paralleled by two female excesses: the "femina" and
"dependa" poses. While the dependa woman plays a co-
quettish role, the femina woman plays a vamp.

Femina is the literal counterpart of macho: competitive
sexuality gone wild. Femina women are hard drinkers,
loud talkers, and lusty laughers. The femina woman comes
straight at a man like a human avalanche and pats his
bottom, hugs his neck, or sits on his lap. Femina gals roll
their shoulders like Mae West and deport themselves like
Miss Piggy. The femina guise is competitive. Women
match women for male attention with ever more radical
signals. Hemlines rise, necklines plunge, bras push higher,
and colors brighten; hot pinks, electric greens, fiery reds,
and ultrascarlets vie for men's eyes. Perfumes go on heavier,
eye shadow goes on darker, mascara goes on thicker, and
so forth, until the femina costume eventually swallows a
woman whole.

The problem with femina women, apart from the threatening hard sell, is that they violate an all-important courting maxim: the principle of *exclusion*. A man needs to feel
that a woman can be *his*. His alone, truly and only his.
The femina woman defies the need and acts as if she is
interested in the whole male category, in generic maleness.
Her behavior suggests that any representative of the masculine gender will do. It's saturation advertising.

At the other extreme stands dependa woman. If femina
is the counterpart of macho, dependa is macho in reverse.
Dependa is the quiet, shrinking-violet pose some women

use in courtship. Men are patsies for dependa performances, which first lure by activating a man's protective instincts and then trap by leading him into an unfair game of "What's wrong?"—"Nothing."

If anything, dependency displays work too well in courtship. A woman who sits demurely in one spot all evening fanning herself, waiting like a geisha, will soon draw a man. But the "meek" act only limits her range of choices, because she won't have an easy time getting rid of the first man who sits down beside her. And she won't add much to the relationship. In fact, dependa women eventually suck out a man's energy (with "What's wrong?" —"Nothing") and pull him into an emotional vortex where the courtship turns pouty, whiny, and manipulative.

Courtship is negotiation, not control. Femina and dependa guises manipulate impressions by concealing more than they reveal. If personality doesn't show through her act a woman might as well peel off the costume, prop it up like a Raggedy Ann doll, and go home. Men want to see the woman behind the role.

So how can a woman fulfill a man's expectations? To begin with, although the Sally Field persona is an effective one, imitating her won't work. The point is simply to show *yourself*.

It's perfectly alright to take the initiative with a man. Dare to be bold: utter the first words. You might have to, because a strange thing can happen in courtship, a subtle reversal of roles. Victor Hugo noticed the turnabout more than a hundred years ago when he wrote, "The first symptom of love in a young man, is timidity; in a girl, it is boldness." Far from thinking you too forward, a man will be thankful you broke the ice. Remember that his macho side is for other men; around you he may lock up.

But don't do what some women do and overcompensate for nervousness with nonstop talking. Give him a chance to say something early in the conversation. Don't fear the

dead air of silence. Look at the man, smile, and wait—
doing so will show confidence. This subtle linguistic pause
is a potent device that can draw a person in. When you
pause keep your eyes turned on the partner's face and
smile for the whole three seconds, which is all it takes to
tease a response.

Carefully monitor your nonverbal behavior during the
crucial opening ten seconds of an interaction, that is,
during the "first-impression" stage. Resist the temptation
to cover your mouth with your hand (hand-over-mouth is
an aversive signal). Preen your hair instead. Run your
fingers through the tresses and push them off one side of
your face. Hair-preening is a prime cue.

Make sure you've turned your body directly toward him
and lean slightly forward. After a warm, three-second eye-
to-eye gaze and the hair-preen, gaze down and synch into
an alternating gaze-contact–gaze-downward pattern. Stand
up straight, relax your shoulders, keep your chest out and
your tummy in, and slightly arch your back. Make a
special effort not to compress or tense your lips or to show
your tongue. Practice in front of a full-length mirror.

A word about how to address a man. Men, one study
showed, like and feel liked more by women who use their
first names in a conversation. So don't hesitate to call a
man by his given name once or twice to make the relationship seem more familiar. (A man who uses a woman's first
name too early, though, is apt to seem "phony.")

Experiment with a technique known as *active listening*.
A man likes to think that what he says is weighty and
substantial. (The same goes for women.) Never mind if
what he says is in fact trivial. The gist of active listening,
which is a proven business-management technique, is to
draw a person out by gesturing *as you listen*. "Don't just
stand there" sums it up. So give his power-hungry ego a
boost. Cant your head over to one side, nod, purse your
lips thoughtfully, raise your brows when he makes a key

point, and so on. Don't butt in, don't even say, "Yes," or, "Uh-huh," until he finishes. Just give rapt attention and a reflective stream of "I see" gesticulations. Watch them register on his importance meter.

Men are simple creatures. All a woman need do to court is pump up the male ego. Give him something he likes to talk about; then remain silent. Let him get it all out before taking a turn. When he's finished, pause three seconds before replying, then inflate his importance gauge to the maximum and pose a question. Nothing flatters a man more than a request that he display his knowledge, such as it is. Oh, you can argue with him—if you think getting it all down on the permanent record is more important than courting. But flattery will get you further than the truth will.

Anything you do or fail to do will register in the courtship centers of a man's limbic brain. He's taking it all in. Overall, the best policy is to behave as you feel. That is, after you've flattered your partner and you hear the little voice in your head asking, "Should I or shouldn't I?"—go with the former. Showing, not inhibiting, is the most promising route in courtship. The worst signal is no signal.

Above all, be happy around men. The easiest way to persuade a man you're beautiful is to light the room with your smile. That expression adds three points to any face: a "seven" becomes a "ten." Deep in the male psyche is the presumption that a woman will so enjoy his company, that she'll feel so happy in his radiant zone, that her pleasure will register as an uncontrolled grin. Of course it's unreasonable, but that's the nature of courtship. A man interprets signals of glumness and deadpan looks personally. He'll consider himself a failure unless he makes you happy.

A Man's Woman, a Woman's Man

These are picky times. Millions of men and women are waiting for the perfect mate. They go into exact detail telling you what they want. "We don't want much," three fed-up young women wrote in a Valentine's Day letter to the editor, "just a man with class, intelligence, and wit, who is caring, affectionate, and communicative. Come out wherever you are! Don't hide. Be a woman's man!" All three in their twenties, the women wrote in exasperated tones about the lack of any good men, the dearth of men who combined even two of these traits.

"What do I want?" a thirty-five-year-old divorced mother of two mused as I switched on the tape recorder. "Energy, sincerity—a personality wouldn't hurt—he should be an easy conversationalist. I'd hope he could express his feelings; I don't like silent types. And, let's see, well, he should give me flowers every now and then and write love poems in cards." She might have added, "Clean hands and eyes that glint like sequins," if we hadn't gone right to the main issue: Where are such mates? Why are they so hard to find?

If you think women are choosy, look at what men say they want. "Simple," one unmarried thirty-year-old told me. "She's gotta be attractive, but more than that. She'll have to be *alive,* have lots of energy and enthusiasm. And her own opinions. And intelligence, naturally, so we can talk. And . . . let's see . . . yeah, she has to be happy, stable. It would really help, too, if she liked the Dallas Cowboys. . . ."

But talking about ideal partners and finding the right candidates are as different as dreaming of wealth and being rich. Two days after the Valentine letter appeared in the paper a man answered with his own version of, "Where have all the good mates gone?" Disputing the lack of good men, the writer countered with the claim that classy, intelligent, and witty women are equally hard to find. Then the swift close: "Real men *do* exist—we're out there, everywhere, looking for *you,* trying to get in touch with a real man's woman."

Claims and counterclaims. The bottom line is that people are choosier today. There are some things going on above the line, too—for one, the mismatched babyboom figures, with not enough older men for older women, nor sufficient younger women for the younger men. That, and some grim arithmetic: single women aged 30 to 54 outnumber men in the same range by about 128 to 100. But we can let sociologists worry about statistics. All this bemoaning the lack of qualified men and women is really good news.

Good indeed, because all anyone serious about courtship needs to do is *exhibit* the sought-after traits. "Energy," "enthusiasm," "happiness," "caring," and "class" reduce without remainder to nonverbal signals. "Affectionate" and "communicative" map right onto the behavioral signals listed in this chapter. To seem "sincere" you must act yourself. Square up your torso, gaze eye to eye, lean forward, and smile. Don't sit back and leave things to chance. Writing letters won't help. As one anonymous sage put it, "Luck is a very good word, if you put a *p* before it."

Quiz

- Despite video dating, radio call-in shows, and computer matching, it's likely to be as hard trying to make face-to-face contact in the 1980s as it was back in the nineteenth century. True or false?
- When talking with your date on the phone you can pick up more emotional nuances if you listen with:
    a. Your left ear.
    b. Your right ear.
    c. Either ear—it doesn't matter.
- Only one of the following items is likely to grow in importance in the courtship of the '80s:
    a. Androgyny.
    b. Unisex.
    c. Cosmetic surgery.

11

Courting in the Future

> *I'm tired of the past and even the future's beginning to seem repetitive.*
>
> —*JOHN LYDON OF THE SEX PISTOLS*

David told Simon he loves Carol, and she told him to get lost. Robert smooched Barbara, who threatened to quit if he did it again. Val blew up when Larry had Jim confess his love for Kathy. Julie gave Pamela's wedding dress to Ann. Barbara ordered Leslie to become a surrogate mother; Leslie went away. Steven got mad when Charles and Edgar became closer to Diane. Gene called John and threatened to tell Charlotte that Sarah is out to steal Tom. Sally made another pitch for George. Drew blamed Debra for the breakup between Yvonne and Terry, while Terry swore never to forgive Marlissa for back-stabbing Jon. Jack went out with Jill.

Analyze all the convoluted story lines of the television soap operas and you'll find strong courtship themes. In fact, the same syrupy plots fuel most movies. Even high-brow drama, like the "Masterpiece Theater" production of Tolstoy's *Anna Karenina*, is little more than variations on boy-meets-girl.

Courtship, you could say, makes the world go round. But where is the mating game headed? What will love signals look like in the future, say in the next ten to one hundred years?

Before we begin forecasting, let's be clear about where we stand *now*. "Now" changes daily, but the cutting edge of the present is apparent to anyone who leafs through *People* magazine's 1983 New Year's issue. Here we'll find all the current folk beliefs and customs likely to bear on courtship through the rest of the '80s.

Over the course of six thousand years of recorded history, little has changed. In the picture-filled pages of *People*, courtship present looks a lot like courtship past. Consider:

Here's Diana Ross dressed in animal stripes, her thighs bared and her neckline plunging to her navel, giving us Lauren Bacall's coy look. And here we see actor Kevin Kline on a bed giving Meryl Streep his best *en face* gaze, microns away from her nose. Moving on, it's Ronald Reagan standing behind his presidential desk in a "power" suit, holding the premier symbol of masculinity, a football, triumphantly over his head. And here's Joan Jett, "rock's latest leading lady," with her lips and eyes heavily made up and her nose cosmetically scaled down, wearing an eye-catching striped top.

There's more. Staring straight at you off the page, hands resting boldly on his hips, football's Heisman Trophy winner Herschel Walker has his shirt off and four gold chains around his neck. The nude model for Caress soap has her face tipped shyly downward, her eyes almost shut, her shoulders submissively raised, and she's touching herself—the pink bar of soap juxtaposed against her soft skin seems more feminine than it would stuck in Herschel Walker's belt or held aloft by Mr. Reagan's passing arm.

Courtship signals still sell products, as we see in the Barclay ad, where that granite-jawed man seductively eyes a woman, giving her his best coy look as he lights a cigarette. And the Mustang ad with the pinstriped court-shipmobile in the foreground and in the background the man leaning close to a woman standing against a tree—well, the limbic suggestion is clear: let Ford speed you down the wooing path.

For anyone who finds sameness unexciting, the court-ship beliefs and customs seen in *People*'s pages must seem dull: the same gestures with the same seductive meanings. Here's the Reverend Sun Myung Moon wearing religious-white vestments and a star-encrusted crown that makes his head look more powerful. Moon is performing a mass marriage for more than two thousand couples—a clear demonstration of his power—and he's done alright in court-ship himself, with two wives and thirteen children . . . so far.

Miss America for 1983, Debra Sue Maffett, had her face made more babylike with a nose job, we're told. Before the operation, the tip used to droop. . . .

And so it goes. Looks, infantilism, power, masculinity, and femininity—as much a part of courtship now as they ever were. And we can look ahead to more of the same in the 1980s and beyond. Paris fashion designers predict that women's clothes will cling to the curves this year. A safe bet, but nothing new. *Octopussy*, the James Bond picture starring Roger Moore, has the same winning combination of sex and violence previous Bond films have had. And *Superman III*, in which the Man of Steel falls in love with his high school sweetheart, reinforces our most popular totem belief—that the perfect match is between beauty and power. King Kong is alive and well.

Is there nothing new under the sun? The educated an-swer in courtship is, in a word, ''No.'' Our wooing prac-tices will proceed much as they have for decades—for millennia, in fact—unless something drastic happens to the biological heart of sex itself. Two thousand years from now, if mating somehow shifted, so would courtship signaling. And if the courting paradigm changed, social life as we know it would disappear.

In the 1960s certain worked-up intellectuals talked about "free love." Many felt that after the much-publicized "Sexual Revolution" men and women would automatically have quicker courtships, lighter commitments, more mates, and unlimited sex. Men's eyes glazed over as they thought about "free sex." The idea was to walk up to an attractive woman, wink, and make love on the spot.

An odd thing happened on the way to the Revolution. People talked a lot about sex, and attitudes did liberalize somewhat—but courtship stayed the same. Daring couples experimented with swinging sex, but then gave it up. They found themselves irresistibly focusing in on one mate above the others and desiring, in spite of abundant "free sex," to sequester that special person away from the eyes and trespassing gropes of fellow swingers.

New Ways to Meet Mates

Courtship in the 1980s is as rigorous as ever. If anything, progressing through the phases is harder now thanks to electronic techniques that make it easy to screen thousands of partners *out*. Just depress the computer's "Sort" button, and without seeing a single tummy-tuck, head-tilt, or smile you can say no to entire categories of would-be mates.

Despite the much-touted sexual revolution, it's as hard to make face-to-face contact now as it was in the nineteenth century, when exaggerated etiquette had people drape their table legs, segregate books by the authors' sex, discourage old maids from sleeping in rooms that had men's portraits on the walls, and avoid erotic phrases like "the naked eye." Indeed, personal contact is even more difficult today because men and women of the '80s increasingly go through the first three phases of courtship *alone*.

TV

Take video dating. You sit in front of a camera, make a five-minute tape of yourself courting, and go home. The tape stays behind in a video library and courts *for* you. A coach advises what colors look best on you, suggests which gestures convey an effective image, and helps you prepare a script. To discourage lying, dissuade married men, and keep out psychopaths, TV courting parlors verify IDs, addresses, and phone numbers, and advertise their services as "private and safe."

Video dating takes courtship's essential obliqueness one step further. The medium "decouples" courter from courtee, thereby reducing the natural insecurities of the first meeting. It's an electronic version of the go-between, the paid intermediary or matchmaker who has been used for generations in traditional societies.

Pay your fee (steep: about $350), browse through printed biographies, and call up images on the screen. Watch in total privacy until someone's love signals strike the right chord, and the staff will invite that candidate to view *your* tape. If there's a resonance, a tape-to-tape attraction, your courtship has an electronic headstart into Phase Three.

Of the novel high-tech resources of the '80s, video dating is perhaps the most true to life, because it's the most nonverbal. For anyone with special problems—say, no date in three months, and you've been trying—it's worth spending $350 to go through the routine. Even if you never call anyone, seeing yourself "perform"—and contrasting your presentation of self with "rival" tapes others of your sex have made—is worth more than the fee.

Choosing a costume, a hairstyle, a script, and the right

nonverbal attitude, as well as the feedback coaches give
you and the chance to go through several "takes," will
make all the courtship signals we've seen more real. Seeing
your own head-tilts, lip-bites, shoulder-shrugs, brow-raises,
head-tosses, gaze-aversions, palm-rotations, and so on will
put you in the proper mindset to begin thinking of ways to
improve your courting "pose."

It's a powerful advantage to see yourself as others see
you. You'll never watch an actor again without finding
gestures and mannerisms to try. Don't think of it as
imitating, but like learning new words. Your expressive-
ness improves with each added nonverbal signal, because
in courtship, posture is power.

Radio

Call-in dating over the radio waves began in 1976, and
today several American cities have courtship talk shows.
Dial the staton, and if you're lucky enough to get through—
less than 1 percent do—you tell about yourself and what
you'd like in a mate. Then you give out your phone
number and wait. Stations screen the calls they broadcast,
but confidentiality is breeched every time they air a home
phone number.

Apart from the fact that predatory married men and
weirdos might call you, phone-in dating has some merit.
More revealing personal information comes over a phone
than most people realize. The brain can process an
astounding amount of emotional data through auditory
channels. In other words, we have an ear for feelings and
can expertly read tempo, loudness, hesitations, throat-
clearings, and tone of voice as signals of mood.

Because the right brain hemisphere of right-handed people is the "musical," the intuitive, side, it's good strategy
for these persons to listen to callers through the *left* ear.

(Nature got the anatomical wires crossed: our left ear connects to the right side of our brain.) If you're left-handed, use the right ear. The less-dominant, "feeling" hemisphere is better at decoding the emotional nuances carried in human speech.

Phone dating gets you immediately to Phase Three. But while it reaps the benefits of conversation, the eventual face-to-face meeting can be psychologically jarring. Our brain constructs a definite mental image of strangers on the phone. Specific traits—height, weight, body shape, nose size, hair color, and even eye color—come into focus on the brain's screen, because the unfamiliar voice reminds us of someone we know.

The caller never looks the way we imagined, and the mismatch can be disconcerting. This incongruency is what led hundreds of women to raise their brows and bring their hands to their mouths in shock when they laid eyes on Bachelor Number . . . *Three*. On "The Dating Game" men sometimes sounded like Riccardo Montalban but looked like Tattoo.

No one should feel unworthy using an electronic dating aid. Meeting mates has always been a test of nerves. Some astronauts fear courtship more than they do piloting spacecraft; many movie stars have said that going on "The Tonight Show" is easier than going out on dates. Burt Reynolds confessed he would be "petrified" to go to a singles' bar. Any technique, therefore, that gets a person to the Conversation Phase without psychic damage has merit.

Computer Matching

Scientists have not yet built an emotional computer. No one has written a program that would allow an IBM processing unit to rant, rave, fume, sigh, and shut itself down in disgust. So computer dating is almost a contradiction in terms. There's just no reasonable, programmable way for partners to project their feelings through silicon circuits.

It's too neocortical, too logical, too *sane*. You fill out a structured questionnaire on the assumption that you *already* prefer, say, a five-foot-six, red-haired Anglo to a six-foot, brown-haired Asian. But if anything, courtship is exploratory, highly experimental. You test and endure, encounter and bear an assortment of partners until experience teaches what's best.

So don't expect computer circuitry to match you with the right person. You might as well forget the other traits and just enter "male" or "female" (and "nondrooler") on the form and go out with a variety of people. No amount of machine-readable data can tell you what thirty seconds of nonverbal signals can, so you may as well leave the list of "preferred traits" blank. All a computer can do is pair you with another person who wants to go out.

Classifield-Ad Dating

DANTE HAD A VISION, BEATRICE. I'll be happy with a down-to-earth friend who knows herself. Sincere, educated gentleman, good sense of humor, diverse cultural interests, thirty-eight-years old. My medical practice with children and families reflects my belief in their importance. I would appreciate hearing from sincere, intelligent ladies, mid-twenties to early thirties. Please write. . . .

Indeed. For $25 and up you can run an ad in *Intro*, a singles' magazine. It's safe—you're assigned a box number—and if you wind up dating a homicidal maniac, don't worry: the magazine will have his address and phone number on file for the local police.

No wooing device should be dismissed out of hand, but classified-ad dating offers the least-reliable meeting cues of any of the modern techniques. You list a number of questionable, subjective, easily falsifiable traits—"blonde," "cute," "tall," "dark," "bowler," "jazzerciser," "forty but firm," "millionaire," "saint"—and interested parties get in touch by letter. Two handwritten pages are a good reply, and you go from there.

Ad dating is the simplest way to say, "I want a partner," without exposing yourself. In effect, you hide behind the printed word. Prisoners use the technique when they advertise in college papers for co-ed pen pals. Because each classified ad reaches hundreds to hundreds of thousands of readers, you can't help getting replies. It's a version of the numbers game, like broadcast fertilization. Scatter yourself widely enough and reproduction is guaranteed.

But it's quality you're really after, not quantity. Courtship is a process of one person revealing himself to another. You can delay—put your image on videotape, phone it in, or allude to it in a letter—but sooner or later boy-meets-girl boils down to human beings trading signals in overlapping personal zones. In the foreseeable future, courtship will still be face to face.

"Trust No Future, Howe'er Pleasant!"

Longfellow's caution notwithstanding, we can be certain that all the traditional love signals—clothing signals, hourglass figures, strong hands, palm-rotations, smiles, etc. —will continue working for the rest of this millennium, at least. These are courtship's good old days. Yet, an artificial heart has been successfully implanted in a Seattle dentist's chest as these words are written, and who can say what strange galaxy of prosthetic devices looms on the medical horizon?

WOOING TO END,
SCIENTISTS SAY

NEW LOS ANGELES. Feb. 14, 3000 (AP)— Researchers at the U.S. Department of Reproduction announced today that snap-on sexual organs will become available for sale to the general public on March 1. Scientists at University Hospital here, who have been testing the controversial snap-fitting genital devices since 2983, say most users prefer the bionic parts to the original organs.

"Sex is easier," one patient said, "because while your snap-ons make love you can stay home and eat or watch TV." Organ hosts pair their devices in special heart-shaped "love chambers" in the Poconos. The Reproduction Department anticipates that separating sex from the body will allow citizens to work harder because they will spend less time preening, showing off, and pitching woo.

Let's hope technology never goes that far. If sex ever *is* divorced from the body, courtship signaling would drastically change. There would be little need for fashionable clothes, swaggering, makeup, or gender contrast. Freed from the burden of attracting mates, the human body would lose most of its charm. But it's not likely to come to this anytime soon.

However, here are a few small changes that *are* likely in the courting code.

Cosmetic Surgery

As the face ages it begins to look tired. The nose enlarges and droops. Lines deepen, and the face takes on a meaner, more-threatening look. Loose "turkey-gobbler" folds come into the neck, which tends to age early, erasing one's clean jawline. Muscle tissue beneath the skin of the eyelids thins, allowing fatty tissue to poke through and create puffed, weary-seeming eyes. Ears and earlobes keep growing throughout life.

Look forward to men and women using plastic surgery more routinely to restore the youthful courtship signals of their faces. Surgical techniques are becoming ever safer and more sophisticated. It's possible now to augment the cheekbones and chin, reduce the nose, take out turkey-gobbler folds, smooth eyelid wrinkles, pin back the ears, reposition the jaw, repair "drooped eyebrows," and lift the face.

In the future, expect men and women to have a bigger selection of facial traits to choose from. Just as certain canons of beauty and facial proportions discovered in antiquity, such as the basic T shape classical brows make with a straight nasal bridge, will stand, it's unlikely that standards of attractiveness will change significantly. "Schadow's angle," for example, the angle between the upper lip and the bottom of the nose, will remain in the 90-to-95 degree range in the most alluring faces. You can assume, therefore, that people undergoing rhinoplasties fifty years from now will choose the 90-degree right angle over either a "hook" (less than 80 degrees) or "pug" (more than 100 degrees) look.

Paycheck Power

One measure of masculinity in America is the size of a man's paycheck. Money is power, and in courtship to be outearned is to be undervalued. Increasingly, some women earn more than men. In about one-tenth of American working couples women now bring home fatter checks.

More monetary power for women could stand the traditional courting paradigm on its head. There aren't enough secure men around to take such a role reversal without experiencing the stress of diminished sex drive, psychological abuse, or divorce, all of which researchers say already plague couples with higher-earning wives.

Major adjustments will be needed. But it's hard to say how easily men will give up the power edge they've enjoyed for so long in the mating game. Men traditionally "marry down." Which is to say, they choose partners who are less educated and less "successful" than themselves. And problems are brewing already. Highly successful women are having severe difficulties finding mates. When you hear of doctors marrying nurses, you know, for the most part, which sex is M.D. and which is R.N.

The most likely way out of upside-down courtship is for older women to begin pairing with younger men. That's happening more frequently, but don't look for any large-scale changes in power relations between the sexes in courtship. "Taller," "heavier," "older," and "richer" are likely to persist as prime masculine traits.

Androgyny

There's little chance that the signals of masculinity and femininity will change. As a fashion, the unisex look died a decade ago. Any style that obscures or plays down the differences between men and women is bound to fail. When Dick starts looking like Jane, Jane starts looking at Bob. . . .

If you've kept up with recent theorizing about the sexes (if you've read, say, Herb Goldberg's *The Hazards of Being Male* or June Singer's *Androgyny)* you've heard the belief expressed that, sometime soon, men and women will act more alike and see the world in the same light. Men will exercise their feminine side, and women will actualize their male potential, and the two genders will have fewer basic misunderstandings about life. And live happily ever after.

Maybe so, but I doubt it. There's a difference between understanding how the other sex thinks, on the one hand, which we truly are coming to appreciate, and actually *thinking alike,* on the other. Far from converging, in the future men and women may *diverge* as they become even more secure in their sexual roles.

Look for women to be more feminine in the political and social worlds of the 1980s. Take business. Watch the women's three-piece "success suit" become less masculine/strength oriented and more feminine/showy as women find they can be powerful *and* flamboyant at the same time. No one will tell the company president to wear a Brooks Brothers suit if she'd rather wear a blue satin dress. The feminine presence will flower in its own way in the corporate world of the future.

Presently, the only men who remove "embarrassing" hair, wear lipgloss, mascara, and teased hairdos, and dance in kick lines are those who gear their courting routines to other men. A man frequently must beam out a flurry of feminine signals to lure another man near, given male competitiveness.

In courtship, androgyny looks like a dead end.

Don't Panic

Things are changing fast, much too fast. There's a fresh
syndrome in the psychiatric jargon, "neophobia," fear of
anything new. But courtship is safe from the changes
exploding all around us. In fact, courtship is refreshingly
conservative. You can depend on it staying the same.
What attracts today will attract just as strongly tomorrow.

Quiz

- Courtship is:.
    a. Serious and solemn.
    b. Playful.
    c. A matter of signals.
    d. All of the above.
- When Casanova entered a room he looked for a woman's:
    a. Trembling hands.
    b. Beckoning eye.
    c. Shy smile.

12

Conclusion—The Joy of Courting

Love and a cough cannot be hid.
—*HERBERT*

We have looked at love as a form of comunication and studied its signals. Just as a fever is symptomatic of disease, shoulder-shrugs, head-tilts, and pouts are symptoms of love. It's no accident that Arthur Conan Doyle, the creator of Sherlock Holmes, was trained as a physician by one of Europe's foremost medical diagnosticians. Holmes's genius for minutia, for reading volumes from the commonplace, from bootlaces, for example, or sleeves, comes from medicine.

Call them signals, symptoms, or clues, all the courtship behaviors we've looked at are always there, available for the reading. One merely has to open the book, as it were, to piece together the tale. With the first gesture you're privy to how people really feel about each other.

Overall, the tone of this book has been light, because that stance best reflects courtship's playful nature. It doesn't matter that sex and romance are serious or that men and women take monumental life-and-death risks for the sake of love. Wooing itself is frisky and fun.

The puckish little boy or the impish little girl is what we like in prospective mates. Silliness draws us close; solemnity sets in *after* the courtship. When the giggles are gone you know you're over the hump and on the boundless plain of the long-term relationship. We make light of marriage, but wooing urges us toward commitment whether we reach it or not.

As Emerson taught us, "Love is strongest in pursuit; friendship in possession." Courtship is a means to an end. You trade advertisements and hope for truth, but in the early stages of boy-meets-girl eagerness to please may exaggerate the claim that you're right for each other. So read the signals cautiously and take heed.

There *is* a Ms. or Mr. Right for each of us, or at least several people who would be better for us than most of the rest. So we must court a variety of candidates and savor the clues. Unless it's love at first sight—the rare flash of recognition that comes when all the cues go off simultaneously—you owe yourself a copious courtship. Which is to say, take your time.

Casanova used to walk through rooms looking for women with trembling hands. Quavering fingers revealed that a woman felt excited, and a bit scared, at the prospect of having an affair. The shakiness told Casanova that she was in the palm of his hand.

Indeed. Courtship signals are powerful. And the longer you study them the more you'll agree that a wooing metaphor permeates the entire social fabric. We court teachers, bosses, and friends as well as lovers. An understanding of love signals will take you to the heart of sociability, to the deepest unexpressed motives. Enjoy yourself, enjoy others. That, in the end, is what it's all about.